Seven Ways
to Treat a Lady

Confessions of a Bartender

. . . .

Joseph Palmese

DORRANCE
PUBLISHING CO
EST. 1920
PITTSBURGH, PENNSYLVANIA 15222

The events, people, and places herein are depicted to the best recollection of the author, who assumes complete and sole responsibility for the accuracy of this narrative.

Dorrance Publishing Co
701 Smithfield Street
Pittsburgh, PA 15222
Visit our website at *www.dorrancebookstore.com*

ISBN: 978-1-4809-0887-1
eISBN: 978-1-4809-0749-2

Contents

• • •   • • •   • • •

Prelude

. . . .

I was eighteen when I was forced to make a difficult decision…the court-or-dered probation and possible jail time or enlist in the military were my only two options. After careful consideration, I felt it would be safer enlisting than trying to live at home (and the thought of going to jail truly scared me to death). The decision was also aided by my father, who was threatening to "kill" me if I continued on the path that I was on. I had made some really stupid decisions, but because of my age, I was still considered a "youthful of-fender"…so I still had choices.

My cousin, "Junior," stood six feet, six inches tall, weighed in at around 300 pounds, and there wasn't an ounce of fat on his body. He was standing between my dad and me, in an effort to keep me alive. With only the use of one hand, he pressed me against the wall, holding me almost a foot off the ground. He was waiving the other hand in my father's face, telling him not to hit me anymore. As I mentioned, I considered it safer to join the military than try to live at home. *I enlisted in the US Marine Corps the fol-lowing morning.*

After intense "boot" camp training at Parris Island and flight training in Pensacola, Florida, I received my orders and headed out to my first permanent duty station—El Toro Marine Base in Southern California.

. . . .

I had been there for about three months when I decided to move in to a small apartment off base. My new "bachelor" apartment was one of only eight in the complex, but it was clean and pleasant, and, as I quickly found out, *I had neighbors.*

In the seven apartments remaining, there were ten single women. Four college students, three waitresses, a bartender, a bank teller, and a recent divorcee looking for work. The youngest in the group was nineteen and the oldest was a twenty-six-year-old divorcee...eight apartments...ten single women...and me. Just when I thought I had died and gone to heaven, reality hit. What do you get when you combine ten, single, beautiful women with a very young, nineteen-year-old marine? A girls' club with a bodyguard, busboy, waiter, and part-time slave—all rolled up into one very innocent boy. US Marine Corps or not, *I wasn't a "man" just yet.*

They would lounge around in their nightgowns, shorts, T-shirts, underwear, basically, in whatever was comfortable...and sit for hours, talking trash about all the men in their lives. In the entire time I lived there, I was never considered more than just one of the "girls." I needed to find a part-time job and get the hell out of there—quick...these girls were *destroying* my ego.

• • •   • • •   • • •

After finishing up a long day on base, I was feeling a little restless, and more than just a little lonely; so before heading to my apartment, I decided to sample a few of the local bars in the area. I found one that I particularly liked, the Red Turtle. It was dark, but comfortable, and it was starting to get busy. I made my way to the bar, found a stool close to the waitress station, and settled in. I was extremely nervous as I ordered my first drink; after all, the drinking age in California *was* twenty-one, and I had just celebrated my eighteenth birthday.

The bartender placed my scotch in front of me and I started to watch him work his magic; I was mesmerized, as he was in complete control of his surroundings. I noticed that the live entertainment had started, but I couldn't stop admiring the way the bartender worked the room. Before I knew it, the lights were turned up, and I heard the dreaded words—"last call."

As I watched the bartender, "Joe P.," started to close out the outstanding bar tabs, I realized that the four beautiful women sitting at different places along the bar were all there for the same reason. Patiently waiting for the bartender to decide which one of them would be lucky enough to go home with him...*and here I thought that they weren't talking to me because of my haircut.*

• • •   • • •   • • •

A few days later, I stopped by again and "Joe P." was very cordial, and remembered my drink (he still hadn't asked my age), and I fast became a "regular" customer.

Joe took a liking to me, especially when I shared my desire to become a bartender and that I wanted him to be my teacher. The Red Turtle was a nightclub close to both my apartment and the marine base, and when Joe told me that they were looking for help, I immediately applied for and accepted a position as their doorman, because, as I mentioned, I did have that "bodyguard" physique.

• • • • • • • • •

His name is Joe P., my name is Joe P., and that's where the similarity ended. He was twenty-six years old, six feet, two inches tall, and weighed 165 pounds. I was eighteen years old, a little shy of five feet seven, and I weighed 225 pounds. He put on his Stetson hat and cowboy boots, and looked like he walked right out of the Marlboro Man poster. I put on my gold chains and medal, unbuttoned the top three buttons of my black shirt, and looked like I should be somebody's bodyguard. The women surrounded him, and worked very hard trying to give him their phone numbers. The women surrounded me, because I was his friend, and they all wanted *his* phone number.

• • • • • • • • •

For the next three weeks, I would go to work an hour early just to watch Joe set up the bar. He enjoyed teaching his new protégé and answered all of my questions without hesitation. He would usually start his shift at around three o'clock to get the bar "set up," and Beth, his cocktail waitress, would also get in at around three to get her lounge area ready. I would come in early just to watch and learn; unfortunately, about the only thing I learned was that every day, around three-thirty, both Joe and Beth would disappear into the liquor room—for about twenty minutes. When they came back to the bar, they would be smiling far more than they had a right to. Joe called it his daily "inventory," something I would need to learn if I were serious about getting into the business. Obviously, he was a very conscientious bartender, because the owner of the lounge, as I eventually learned, only required an "inventory" once a month.

A few days earlier, I watched as Joe *had* to choose from the four women waiting for him to get off his shift, and now he was getting "serviced" on a daily basis by his cocktail server. It was then that I became convinced that I had made the right decision to become a *professional bartender.*

I took every opportunity to leave my post at the front door and go to the bar to ask questions, a couple of hours a day, for three weeks. I was feeling pretty good about myself and was sure that I was ready to start my new career.

It hadn't yet occurred to me that you had to be twenty-one years old to serve alcohol in California.

●　●　●　　　●　●　●　　　●　●　●

Not far from my apartment, there was a stretch of bars and clubs specializing in adult entertainment. Since becoming the doorman of the Red Turtle three weeks earlier, I started to meet the other doormen in the area, so it was that when I showed up at a couple of these adult clubs, I was given entrance without any request for my identification (up to this point, it had never occurred to anyone to ask me for my ID—I was a pretty big boy). I was spending a considerable amount of my time off in these establishments, so it was only natural for me to ask the club employees if they knew of any bartending openings; after all, I *had* completed my bartending training in *only* three weeks, and my teacher, my mentor, was an extremely talented *professional bartender.*

The owner of the bar stepped up and told me that he was opening a new club, just down the street, and that if I could start tomorrow, I could have the job. He was in a panic because the bartender he had originally hired for the job took off on a three-day drunk and no one had any clue where to find him. Circe's was opening the following day, and he was in desperate need of a bartender—*and apparently, I was going to be it.*

●　●　●　　　●　●　●　　　●　●　●

It was my first day, it was noon, but as soon as I walked into the club, I lost all track of time. A small, dark room with uncomfortable chairs surrounding a small stage, and, yes, there was a pole in the center of it. A long, sixteen-stool bar was off to one side, and as soon as I stepped behind it, I started to shake. The owner showed me the cash register and I was introduced to the six waitresses/dancers who I would be working with. I realized that I might have been a bit premature in applying for the job, and the fact that I was still just eighteen years old hadn't set in yet. My mentor, Joe, was in the house... he was still in shock that I had the balls to even apply for the job, let alone get it. He thought it would be in my best interest to show up for my first day... just in case I needed a little help. *Thank God he didn't start his own shift at the Red Turtle until four o'clock.*

I was just settling in when Kathy, an extremely attractive, large-breasted woman who was in charge of all the girls, walked up to the waitress station and gave me my first drink order, a bourbon water. It was at this time when Joe P. became my new best friend. I forced myself to slowly walk, not run, to the end of the very long bar, to where Joe had settled, and leaned over to whisper, "What the fuck is in a bourbon water?"

The seasoned and all-knowing bartender just smiled and very quietly offered, "Ice, one and a half ounces of bourbon, water, and try to find a *clean* glass."

I strutted back to the "station" with all of my accumulated knowledge and made the drink. Not a second later, Julie, blond, petite (pure perfection), ordered a Tom Collins, and once again, I reached out to Joe, got the answer, and made the drink. The next three hours were pretty much the same routine, Joe acting as my all-knowing savior while I tried to keep my mind off the almost naked bodies on stage. I was in paradise and hadn't even noticed when Joe left to start his own shift. Fortunately, the rest of my first shift was uneventful and I survived. After all, even *I* realized that our customers weren't there for my personality or the drinks.

For the next three months, my life was looking pretty good. As a marine, I worked split shifts and weekends, and, with just a little notice, could easily manage a four-day shift at the club. My career as a bartender was taking off, and after the first couple of weeks, I was serving a steady stream of regular customers. I was getting to know their drinks fairly well and the extra money was great.

Then there were *my* ladies...scantily clad women, paid to take their clothes off, and I was starting to reap the social benefits. The club was getting busier and management hired a few headliners (professional strippers who put on one a hell of a show twice a night). I no longer gave much thought to the ladies at my apartment complex, but I'm sure that they had no trouble finding a replacement for me.

• • • • • • • • •

I was just setting up my "well," getting ready for a busy Friday, when Kathy showed up in the waitress station with *all* of the girls. She stood there for a few minutes while I tried to stay focused, and looked me square in the eyes. I was still having trouble talking to her eyes and not her breasts...they were just so, so big. But Kathy understood and she was patient. When I finally lifted my eyes, she stated in a very firm voice, "Joseph, you fucked us all." *And I had.* There I was, a very young marine, with some of the best physical training in the world, looking for a place to duck and hide. I was speechless, nervous, with beads of sweat starting to show on my brow, and all I could produce was a pitiful little nod.

How could she have known? I had been discreet, but after all, I was a professional bartender...and I was pretty sure that that was in my job description. As I was starting to lose it, Kathy did something that would stay with me for the rest of my life. She leaned over, just enough to give me a view of her ample cleavage, smiled down at me with that all-knowing smile (you know, the kind that makes the strongest of us melt), and softly said, "Sex with them was just their way of saying thank you, for caring about them, respecting them, and treating them all like ladies."

There was absolutely no way my life could get any better. I was eighteen years young, but because I grew up in New York City, my ego allowed me to think that I could handle just about anything. My military career was to be short lived (only three more years), but I was good at my job, was promoted three times in the last nine months, and I couldn't have asked for a better bartending job.

Apparently, the United States Marine Corps had other plans for me, because the very next morning, I was handed my overseas orders. I was leaving at five o'clock that night for what turned out to be my first of three tours of duty in Vietnam. I had just enough time to pack my duffle bag, tell my landlord I was being shipped out, immediately, and call the owner of Circe's with the news.

I never saw "my girls" again.

The Tender Trap

· · · · · · · · ·

Three years had gone by, thirty-three months of which were in the jungles of Vietnam. To say that I was ready to restart my bartending career was definitely an understatement. I arrived at my new duty station in South Weymouth, Massachusetts, with a chest full of medals, an attitude, and six months left of my military career.

As far as military life goes, my new duty station, the Marine Air Reserve Training Detachment at South Weymouth, was a "walk in the park" compared to the "police action" of Vietnam. Two days a week, Saturday and Sunday, our "weekend warriors" (as our civilian reserves were fondly referred to) would charge onto the base and pretend to be soldiers during the weekend, then go back to their family, friends, and real jobs by Monday morning. Monday through Friday, I was pretty much on my own (it must have been the US Marine Corp's way of saying thank you for the thirty-three months they kept me in a combat zone).

While in combat, a soldier's income is tax free (one of the few perks of going to war), and I had been very lucky in the card games that I hosted while off duty. I left Vietnam with a pocket full of money and a real bad case of "short timer's" attitude (with only six months left in the service and, technically, considered "decorated," based on the number of medals I had on my chest). I didn't give a shit about anything except my bartending career and counting the days till my discharge. In my first week back to the states, I bought a new corvette, rented a small, one-bedroom apartment off base, and set up an interview for a bartending job at a place called the Tender Trap.

· · · · · · · · ·

The Tender Trap was a large nightclub. The actual bar itself was a very long, rectangular affair, located in the front portion of the club. The rest of the room was dominated by a stage, dance floor, and it had a seating capacity for around 300.

Kathleen was the owner, thirty-five years old, a tall, attractive brunette with a very rough, straightforward personality. She looked at my very limited resume and experience, and told me, "Go behind the bar and show me what you got."

The minute I stepped behind the bar, it felt natural. It was like I was at home. Kathleen told me to make a Dirty White Mother, my first drink order in three years, and I just stared at her, with a very stupid, blank look on my face. She told me the ingredients and I apologized. "I'm sorry. In California, it's known as a 'Sombrero.'" I then made the drink.

For the next several minutes, Kathleen threw out drink orders and I managed to make them all without *too* much trouble. I was comfortable behind the bar and it must have showed, because a few minutes later, in spite of my obvious lack of drink knowledge, the boss looked up and proclaimed, "Finally, someone who knows what the hell he's doing back there. Joe, you got the job."

I was back. I still had six months left in the US Marine Corps, but now, I could finally get started on my chosen profession. Kathleen introduced me to her bar manager, Dave, and told me that I could start the next day. My six months at the Tender Trap literally "trapped" me back into the bartending profession I had dreamed about for the last three years. Kathleen was great, and underneath that tough persona beats a heart of gold; she was definitely the "tender" part of the Tender Trap.

She had no interest in teaching me how to make drinks, as she pointed out to me on several occasions that I already proved that I knew how to "fake" making drinks, as was evidenced during my interview. She was more interested in teaching me about the customers in her club; she had them broken down into four groups.

The *regulars*, whom she allowed to enjoy special considerations, including an occasional free drink; the *tourists*, who could be used for interaction with everyone in the bar; the *ladies*, found usually in small groups, looking to have some fun, and hopefully "score" some of those special considerations; and the *men* trying to "score" the ladies.

Kathleen spent a lot of time teaching me about *her* customers. She was a firm believer in "working" the bar, and she informed me that I had been hired more for my personality, not for my limited bartending skills. Kathleen taught me how to mix and match the different groups to keep them all entertained—and coming back for more. She also taught me how important it was to keep the core group of regular customers *and* the ladies happy. The regulars would keep the tourist trade entertained, and the ladies...well, the men will *always* follow the ladies.

• • •   •   •   •   •   •   •

Sandy, a bartender who was quick, smooth, and exciting, was the beautiful blonde who worked the day shift. No one really cared whether or not she could actually pour a drink because her personality was simply awesome. The first time I met her, I asked the impertinent question, "How old are you?"

And she coyly looked over and softly responded, "Old enough to drink... old enough to swallow."

I quickly ordered a scotch; *at the time, it seemed safer than conversation.*

One unusually slow afternoon, I was sitting at the bar, about an hour before my shift started. Sandy seemed to have some personal issues. Every ten minutes, she would run to the bathroom. Pour a few drinks, then run to the bathroom, come back to the bar and pour a few more drinks, run to the bathroom...this went on for what seemed like several hours. It wasn't until she got off of her shift when she finally filled me in. Our bar manager, Dave, and her had been rushing to the bathroom *together*. Pour a few drinks, run to the bathroom, sex with the manager, pour a few drinks, run to the bathroom, sex with the manager—*all* afternoon, and here we all thought that the poor girl was having urinary issues.

• • •   •   •   •   •   •   •

For almost the entire four months I worked at the Trap, I listened to bartender Sandy talk about her pending marriage, and, no...it wasn't to the bar manager. When the day finally came, she took off with her new husband for a two-week Hawaiian honeymoon, and I couldn't wait for her to come back so that she could share *all* the details. Sandy was an anomaly, and for all intents and purposes, she was a shy, young, innocent child, barely old enough to pour a drink. When, in reality, she was one of the kinkiest, nastiest, sexually exciting women I have ever had the privilege to know; she would have some great stories to tell.

I arrived a couple of hours before my shift started, and there she stood, behind the bar, looking, for all intents and purposes, like a conservative, married, old maid...and I wasn't having any of it. I offered to "rent" her bra for the duration of her shift; oh, she could have it back at the end of her shift, but for a hundred bucks, I wanted her braless behind the bar. She gave it almost a minute in thought, and then went to the restroom long enough to take off her bra *and* panties, and handed them to me.

As I handed her the underwear at the end of her shift, she asked me if I could invite one of my friends, Sara, back for a late happy hour. Apparently, there was something about the size of Sara's breasts that Sandy couldn't stop thinking of. *It was nice to have her back. I wondered if her new husband had any clue.*

. . .   .

I was on my way to the Trap to start my shift when I looked over to see a woman in the car next to me smoking a cigarette, and from the way she was handling it, you would think that it was the most intense sensual experience of her life, so I started thinking, and by the time I made it to work, I had a plan. I asked Kathleen if she wouldn't mind if I took a poll of our female bar patrons, and after briefly explaining what I had in mind, it was no problem, as long as I *politely* asked the questions, with a little *respect*, and it would be a great way to jump-start my shift.

I was very polite, and asked only two questions of the women in the bar: "Do you smoke, yes or no? Do you enjoy giving oral sex, yes or no?" Of the one hundred women I had asked, only eight women did not smoke, and of those eight, only two enjoyed giving oral sex. Even with my simple math skills, that meant that I would only have a 25 percent chance of reaping the benefits. Of the ninety-two women who did smoke, ninety enjoyed giving oral sex, which worked out to 97.7 percent opportunity. Obviously, there are *huge* benefits to spending some time with women who smoke.

A few days later, I was sitting next to a guy at the bar on one of my rare days off. He couldn't stop complaining that the woman next to him smelled like smoke. It was obviously bothering him a lot, both physically and mentally. So being the gracious, caring person that I am, I offered to swap places with him. A few hours and a couple of drinks later, only Kathleen understood...*as she watched me escorting the woman out to her car.*

A Few of My Friends

I had a very young, nineteen-year-old "kid" working for me at the marine base. Nathan was my assistant in the operations section of the squadron, but we didn't socialize much on our off time. I wasn't a fan. He was young and not too bright, and that, combined with his looks and attitude, made him a very unassuming "kid," with just one exception: my humble opinion, *he was married to a goddess. I know, but I just spent the last three years in Vietnam—all women were goddesses.*

Julie was eighteen years old, and stood almost six feet tall when wearing her five-inch heels. Her taste in clothes wouldn't put her on anyone's best-dressed list anytime soon, but when she walked into a room, you could almost feel time stop—*she exuded pure sex.*

She was impressive and her breasts were simply amazing, as *only* an eighteen-year-old's *could* be. They were large, with nipples pointing up, as if they were looking right at me, her long, beautifully proportioned legs gracefully make their way to heaven...and then there was her butt, which literally seemed to move as if it had a mind of its own. I was definitely a fan of Julie's. I would use any and all excuses to try to spend time with "both" of them, but they *always* seemed too busy. I would spend many sleepless and lonely nights thinking of that woman.

About a week before I was scheduled to be discharged from the military, Nathan asked me if I wouldn't mind picking Julie up from work. He was having car trouble, and of course, I jumped at the chance. I was told to meet her in a section of Boston that was commonly referred to as the "Combat Zone." The Combat Zone covered an area of about four square blocks, and it was the home to every topless bar and hooker in the city. As I pulled up to the corner to let Julie in, I quickly realized just how naïve I had been. *Julie's work? It was working the streets of the Combat Zone. And Nathan, her husband? He was also her pimp.*

The ride home was pretty silent, and although I was still in shock, I couldn't help but admire the tiny pink panties peeking at me from under her very, very, short skirt. We arrived at her apartment and there was absolutely no way I was going to turn down her invitation to "come in for a drink."

She walked past the small kitchen to her bedroom, pausing ever so slightly to drop articles of clothing along the way. I couldn't keep from admiring the way her ass moved...my eyes were riveted to it, and as those pink panties *finally* found their way to the floor, my whole body was shaking in anticipation.

The only item in the room was a queen-sized mattress on the floor, but by this time, I neither noticed nor cared. I was naked and between her legs in seconds, pumping hard, with my hands firmly attached to those magnificent tits. She quickly flipped me over so that she could ride me...and after a short while, I flipped her over to take her from behind. What seemed like hours was the most intense, sexually charged thirty seconds of my young life, but damn, it sure was fun. After our first contact—and our initial orgasms subsided—we settled down to a much slower pace. I spent the last six months thinking about this and was in no rush to end this quickly.

For a brief, very brief, moment, I *almost* had a tinge of guilt about having sex with the wife of one of my "friends," but that disappeared quickly as our mutual orgasms subsided, and after all, we really weren't friends. It wasn't until I rolled onto the floor, after her third orgasm, that Julie told me that this had been her husband's way of saying good-bye, and to say thank you for being such a good boss. As I have already mentioned, for the last six months, I hadn't considered Nathan much of a friend. Obviously, I should have reconsidered that choice much sooner.

• • •　　• • •　　• • •

It was June 29, and I was scheduled to be discharged from military service on June 30. I packed up everything I owned (my clothes and a digital clock radio), threw them in the back of my corvette, and left, sadly saying good-bye to Kathleen and the Tender Trap.

The colonel in charge of my squadron (my military boss) had scheduled a ceremony for me on June 30, to award me another medal for "surviving" the war...and in hopes of my reenlistment for another six years. I was told that it was a very impressive affair, with the entire squadron (one hundred fifty strong), on the parade grounds...waiting for me, and waiting...but as I already mentioned, I was already gone. I *knew* people, and I had been signed out of the US Marine Corps twenty-four hours earlier.

By the time the colonel realized I was gone, I was halfway across the country on my way back to California to start my new profession.

Hof's Hut

• • •   • • •   • • •

I hadn't spoken with Joe P. in over three years, but he was the only person I knew in California, so I made his apartment my first stop. As fate would have it, he was still living in the same apartment that he had when I left for Vietnam, and he was at home. After his initial shock at seeing me again, he seemed to be ecstatic. He came out to my car to help me with my bags and told me that I could stay for as long as it took me to get settled. He hadn't changed much in the three years that I had been gone, either physically or emotionally, and he was definitely a creature of habit. He lived in the same apartment, still didn't have a serious girlfriend, and was working as a bartender in the same bar; the only change he had made since I left was that he traded his corvette for a Ford Pantera; otherwise, it was business as usual.

Joe decided that to help celebrate my return, he was going to take me out to visit a few local clubs. There I was, back in California for almost six hours, pounding down shots of tequila with beer backs, while watching Joe hustle a couple of beautiful tourists. We were in a nightclub, just a block from Disneyland, and I was told that it was the place where all of the tourists seemed to migrate to after a trip to the "Magic Kingdom." The women, the shots of tequila, Joe hustling, something that came effortlessly to him, it was as if I had never left. I was convinced that I had made the right decision in coming back.

Joe made it a point to subtly remind me that the extent of my bartending experience had been a couple of months spent in a topless bar three years ago, and the last few months spent on the east coast. It was going to be a little tough for me to find a *real* bartending job. "Even good bartenders were having trouble finding jobs."

I listened, knowing that he was just being honest and trying to be kind, but I had spent the last three years thinking about this. We settled in to the drinking aspect of my celebration, and by the end of the night, Joe P. had lined up two women who would be joining our impromptu celebration back at his apartment. *It was good to be back.*

Early the next morning, after the girls left, I picked up a local paper and started dialing for interviews, and with more than just a little luck, I was able to line one up for that afternoon. It was a Hof's Hut on Beach Boulevard in Huntington Beach, one in a restaurant chain of fourteen. It was designed as a unique, high-end coffee shop, combined with a very intimate cocktail lounge. The first thing you would notice as you walk into the lounge area was the sunken bar, shaped like a horseshoe, in the middle of the room. With the actual bar two steps lower than the rest of the room, it allowed the use of armchairs, not bar stools, which gave the room a much more intimate feel, and there were large, custom red booths lining three of the walls. The lounge was kept very dark, with candles providing almost all of the light, and I don't know about the rest of you, but the darker it gets, the better I look. I liked it as soon as I saw the place. My interview was with Burt, the general manager, and I guess my excitement over the look of the place, combined with my un-bridled enthusiasm about bartending, was the right combination, because even with my obvious lack of experience, I got the job.

I went rushing back to Joe's apartment to share my good news with him, but all he could talk about was how he had been able to get me laid on my first day back in California. As far as my new job was concerned, it was a Hof's Hut, a glorified coffee shop and, in his mind, wasn't considered a *real* bar.

$$\bullet \quad \bullet \quad \bullet \qquad \bullet \quad \bullet \quad \bullet \qquad \bullet \quad \bullet \quad \bullet$$

According to Kurt, the bartender put in charge of my training, the original owner had created a very successful operation. He had married the hottest cocktail waitress on his payroll, and was just about to enjoy the fruits of his labor…when he died. Of the fourteen restaurants in his chain, his brother in-herited the two locations in Colorado and his wife of four months received the other twelve, all located in Southern California. She was definitely beau-tiful, and recently rich, but even to my untrained eye, she had no clue on what it was going to take to own and operate her inheritance.

I had been behind the bar for almost an hour when Kurt decided to make it his personal business to show me how to rip off the new owner. He actually enjoyed showing me how easy it was, while she was sitting in the bar, *in front* of the cash register. A quick calculation told me that he was stealing one out of every five dollars that should have found its way into the cash register. *This seemed to be a part of my original bartending "101" training that Joe P. had apparently overlooked.*

Kurt was all about Kurt…the bar would be full, and he decided to set up drinks for the whole bar, on the "house." He would do this several times a night and never charge a customer a dime. At the end of the night, Kurt got tipped very well for giving away drinks, but in reality, it's only a temporary win for him. If a bar isn't making money, eventually, it will close, the owner goes broke, and the entire staff will be looking for work. *Who really wins?* A true professional realizes that it is a "partnership" and that everyone needs to win. If the owner is making money, the increased business means the staff is treated better, and they are making more money, and all will have job stability. *I was young, not stupid.*

My training with Kurt only lasted for three days before I was given my own shift and was introduced to the three, very qualified "older" cocktail servers who would be working with me. Fortunately for me, all three of them seemed to like me and decided to assist the young ex-marine with my next level of training. I wasn't even one year old in "bartending years," so when I say "older," I'm referring to the very attractive, very qualified, seasoned thirty-year-old group of professional servers.

My favorite, Beth, immediately took me under her wing and started to share with me everything she thought I would need to know. From the correct order that drinks should be called out to the bartender to the way I picked up my bottles. During the slow periods in the bar, my training became more intense, and I was soaking it all in. After Beth decided that my basic skills were "adequate," we started to work on my memory, slowly at first, just a few drinks at a time. Beth would pick a table and ask me to make the drinks, and after a while, she would just call out the table number, "table 14," and I would make the drinks, or it would be "table 8, no scotch," or "table 19, no vodka," or just "tables 8, 10, and 12." She was slow and methodical with my training, and it wasn't long before all the servers were ordering their drinks the same way.

Beth kept on me until I was able to remember every drink, at all twenty-four tables, while keeping track of the customers who left and the customers who took their place. To keep me on my toes, once a night, I was asked to recite every drink, for every customer, at the bar and all of the tables…and Beth would tolerate no mistakes.

During each one of my shifts, she would also give me hints on how to handle the difficult customers and how to better serve the good ones. She even bought me several joke books to study, so that I would be able to come up with some quick one-liners to help keep the customers entertained.

There are only four basic reasons to sit at a bar. First, and to some, the most important, you need a drink. Second, the bartender is good looking. Third is the bartender's personality. And fourth, and most important in my mind, is the bartender's abilities (this includes bar knowledge and "bar presence").

The bartender is standing in the "well," listening to his cocktail and food servers while they are ordering their drinks. Using his peripheral vision, he notices from the corner of his eye that a customer is standing patiently, waiting to ask him for some change. The bar is full, with every customer engaged in conversation. If you listen, really listen, you won't necessarily pick out any one conversation, but you can pick out when a customer whispers or raises his/her voice over the "din" of the crowd.

Normally, when customers are trying to order a drink in a busy room, they have a tendency to raise their voices. A good bartender, one who has the presence of mind to be aware of his entire surroundings, whether looking at you or if his back is toward you, will hear this. The servers ordering drinks, the impatient customer waiting for change, the customer at the far end of the bar trying to order another round of drinks, being involved in four conversations at the same time, that is good bar presence. It is a skill that will make a bartender faster and considerably more proficient. "You can teach anyone how to pour a drink, but having good bar presence is difficult, and extremely hard to perfect, but in my opinion, it is extremely important."

I have never considered myself "good looking" and I have no control over the customers who just wanted a drink, so I needed to focus on those areas that I *could actually control—personality and my abilities.*

Before every shift, I would spend an hour "studying" the Old Mr. Boston bar book (the bartender's bible). When I first started, it was my constant companion, not that it was such an interesting read, because it wasn't, but I thought it would be important to remember the different nuances of some of the more popular drinks. I felt that the more I knew, the easier it would be to get a little creative and keep the customers a little excited about their choices. Hard core beer drinkers rarely drank anything but beer, alcoholics have a tendency to stay with what they know, but everyone else looks forward to a little variety.

When reading "Old Mr. Boston" got a little too much for me, I would review the joke books that Beth had purchased, and read them from cover to cover, then back again, to help me memorize the quick one-liners. With the constant assistance and supervision of Beth, I was able to work on my memory skills, drink knowledge, the timing of the quick one-line jokes, and, overall, gave the "perception" of being a good bartender.

• • •   • • •   • • •

It was two in the morning, and I had just finished a very long, hard shift. After we locked up the restaurant, I decided to stop at a local coffee shop close to my apartment for a quick cup of coffee, and to flirt with the girls working the graveyard shift. They were always such a treat to watch, and they all truly enjoyed their job...they had *fun* during their shift. Every once in a while, one of them would return my flirtations, usually Gail, with her tight, little body and long, two-tone hair; it was a great way to end my evening.

As I was sitting at the counter, Angie walked over and sat down next to me. She had just finished her shift at a restaurant down the street, and judging by the look on her face, her shift had been just as tough as mine. As we were enjoying our cups of coffee, she started complaining about her shoulders and neck, and being the true servant that I am, I started to rub her neck. *It was the least that I could do for a fellow professional.* She was just starting to relax, and after a slight moan, I offered to take her back to my apartment, "Just to finish the massage...nothing more, I promise." My apartment was close and we were there in less than five minutes. And five minutes later, she was naked, lying on my bed, face down. I stripped down to my shorts and reached over to get a jar of lotion that I kept in the nightstand next to the bed—*don't ask.*

I started with her feet, slowly moving up one leg until I reached her upper thigh, then the other. I would then move up to her head and work my way down her scalp, her neck, her back, slowly working my way to the sensitive area of her lower back. I worked the muscles hard, and every few minutes, I would reach over to get a little more lotion and then start again, making sure that I warmed the lotion with my hands first. After about an hour, I told her to roll over and I started on her front, with long, smooth, hard strokes, working deeply into her muscles. Once again, I started with her feet, working along one leg at a time, and as I focused on her inner thighs, her pelvic muscles would give me an involuntary twitch closer to my fingers, but I pretended not to notice. I moved back to her head and spent quite a bit of time working the scalp, her facial muscles, and the muscles on each side of her neck. At this point, the word "relaxed" just didn't seem to say enough about her current condition. I moved back to her legs and worked the muscles of her thighs, slowly moving up, working the entire area with a slow, soft, sensuous motion, to within an inch of her pubic hair.

I moved to her breasts. They were small, but well proportioned to the rest of her body, with nipples that were light pink and very sensitive to the touch. I spent a lot of time working them and only left them to continue down her abdomen toward her vagina, when her moans started to get to me, so I pulled back (up until this point, I had been in total control and wanted it to stay that way). Finally, I went back to work and concentrated *only* on the pubic area, and spent quite a bit of time caressing and teasing. I had covered every square inch of her body, at least twice, but I was still planning on honoring what I had promised her at the coffee shop.

The combination of my bartending shift the night before and this massage was starting to affect me physically, and when I looked up at the clock next to the bed, I realized why. It was seven in the morning. I had been working on Angie for almost five hours…and I was done. I slapped her on her ass and told her that it was time that I took her back to her car; she rolled over, stared at me for just a moment, and got dressed. I pulled up next to her car and got out to open her car door. As she stepped out, she turned toward me, looked me straight in the eyes, and slapped the crap out of me. "Next time you get me there, you better finish the job," she said and got into her car and left.

I had spent the last three years of my life in the Orient, and one of the things I took the time to learn was how to massage the woman I was with, in between her orgasms; it was a great way of making sex last longer…much, much longer. Angie was the recipient of some of the things that I had learned while I was in the Orient, and honestly, all I had wanted to do was to just give her a massage.

• • •   • • •   • • •

Years later, my friend Joe P. and I walked into a local establishment for a couple of happy hour beers and introduced ourselves to the bartender working the day shift. He was friendly enough, but when he looked at us sitting next to each other, he started referring to us as "Big Joe" and "Little Joe." My friend is six-two, I am five-seven, but as we sat on the bar stools, we looked as if we were the same height, but because I had much broader shoulders, I was "Big Joe." It wasn't until we stood up that anyone realized how much taller Joe P. was than me, but from that moment on, I don't think I ever stopped calling him "Little Joe."

The shift was changing and our bartender was replaced by a very familiar face. Angie took one look, walked right up to me, took away my beer, and threw me out. Her parting words to me were, "Next time, finish the job." *Obviously, there would never be a next time and some things would never be forgiven.*

• • •   • • •   • • •

Lori was a statuesque woman, forty-two years old, and was probably one of the most beautiful women I had ever seen. If someone had told me that she had just flown in from Paris to make a movie, I would have believed it—she was *that* beautiful. I could not put into words just how happy I was to learn that she only lived a block away from the restaurant and that she was considered one of our best, regular customers. Her favorite spot in the lounge was at the bar, sitting next to the waitress station. I was in heaven. As we got to know each other better, I would take a few moments before the start of my shift to kneel next to her, so that she could massage my back and neck (she had great hands). I had thought that I was pretty good at giving a woman a massage, but Lori made me look like a rank amateur; she would drive her fingers very deep into the soft areas and muscles around my shoulders, and when she was done, I felt like the weight of the world had been lifted from my shoulders. It might not have been considered professional, but *it was a great way to start my shift.*

I had been thinking about changing apartments to move closer to work when Lori offered one of her bedrooms to me. She lived in a large, five-bedroom house with her two daughters, and the maids' quarters were attached to the kitchen; the good news was that they had no maid. It included a bedroom with a small sitting area, a master bathroom, and full access to the kitchen. It sounded perfect, but before I could make a decision, Lori felt that I would need to know a few things about her family.

Lori was one of my best customers. Our conversations had always been light and fun, but she had kept her personal life very private, and I was about to find out why. She had been through a very nasty divorce a few years earlier. She got the house, but had very little money, and needed to find a job. She wasn't interested in giving me all the details. But after a very short time of collecting unemployment checks, she decided to start a modeling career, and to be more specific, *nude modeling.*

Over the last few years, she had become so successful at it that she was able to pay off the mortgage on her home and live quite comfortably. When her daughters saw what mom was up to, they decided to share in the fun and profit as well. As Lori finished telling me her story, she was concerned that I wouldn't be able to handle the fact that mom and her two daughters were nude models, and that they were in the habit of sunbathing in their backyard *nude. Who was I to argue with the photographers who insisted that they have no tan lines?*

It took about a minute and a half to compose myself and tell Lori, with a straight face, that I appreciated her honesty and that I was sure that as long as my bedroom and bath were *isolated*, they would probably never see me; it would be absolutely no problem at all. The next step would be for her to bring in her daughters to meet me, and if they all agreed, I would be able to move in that weekend.

Three nude models, walking around the house, for the most part, naked, and I was going to be living with them…all I would have to do was give a really good first impression to Lori's daughters. The three of them came into my bar the next day. Lori took up her usual position next to the waitress station and started to introduce her daughters, but when daughter number one, Shelly, looked up, she smiled and said, "Hi, Joe. Nice to see you again." Then daughter number two, Sally, chimed in and said, "So this is where you work, Asshole."

I was pretty well screwed. I had met Shelly last week at Joe P.'s bar and I spent a weekend with Sally about a month earlier. It didn't take long for Lori to realize that I already had sex with both of her daughters, and it became very obvious, very quickly, that not only was I not going to be moving in this weekend, I would very probably lose a very good customer. *It is a very small world out there, and that "six degrees of separation" crap that people kept talking about damn near buried me.*

• • •   • • •   • • •

The sole survivor of a very busy night was Patty Ann, a tall, lean brunette who I had come to admire. Her long, flowing hair was highlighted by several blonde streaks and she was wearing a tailored business suit that accentuated a very lithe, athletic body. Her makeup was perfect (*it was always perfect*). She worked at a doctor's office directly behind the restaurant, and would come in often, just to say hi. I was spending a considerable amount of time with her, but neither of us had talked about anything other than a "friendship."

I had just given "last call" and turned the overhead lights on when the "boy toys" showed up. As they took notice of Patty, she took notice of them, and immediately "flipped" her long hair so that it settled across her left shoulder, a very seductive move, and one that she seemed to use whenever she needed attention. As she leaned back in her chair to get a better view of the "boys," they made a beeline to her. The closer they got to her, the more upset I became, and as they took positions on either side of her, I realized that I had feelings for her way past the "friendship" stage.

As they started to put their arms around her, they heard, "Another move closer and I'll break both your arms." They *all* turned to look as I was moving closer to them, with a menacing scowl on my face and a large bottle of Galeano Liquer in each hand.

Patty Ann and I had known each other for only a couple of months, but that didn't seem to stop me. She loved flirting, and was actually very good at it, which was one of the reasons why I was attracted to her in the first place. But obviously, I was ready to take our relationship to the next level, and apparently, I am a very jealous, possessive Italian. I was still young and I wasn't exactly known for my patience. I hadn't yet realized that jealousy was just another way of showing my inexperience and lack of confidence. *I had so, so much to learn.*

• • •   • • •   • • •

After about a year of dating, I asked Patty Ann to marry me, and she accepted. I had been a part of her family for quite a while, but now it was time to take her back to New York, to meet *my* family.

We flew to JFK Airport at six in the morning, and my dad was waiting at the terminal to pick us up. After I introduced Patty to my dad, we walked out to the parking lot to load the car with my one suitcase and Patty's four (we were going to be in New York for almost four days, God forbid she would have to wear an outfit more than once). As my dad pulled up to the exit, the parking attendant started yelling at him, "You stupid, phucking Italian! You pulled too close to the car in front of you! I couldn't get his freakin' plate number!"

Then my dad, being the shy individual that he is, reached behind the car seat and pulled out a police nightstick (always kept there for the little emergencies like this) and started to yell back. "You freakin' spic! Let me out of here before I shove this phucking nightstick up your ass!"

To say that Patty Ann was a little upset would be a "slight" understatement. My mother was a saint to all who knew her, but my dad might have been a bit vocal. As my father pulled out into the flow of traffic, a New York cabbie swerved a little too close and cut us off. My dad chased him down for five blocks, jumped a curb, and swerved a little too close to the cabbie, just to exchange a few choice words before heading home. Patty just covered her head with her coat, curled up into the corner of the car seat, and asked me to please let her know when we got to the house. *Great first impression...it was going to be a very long four days.*

The next day was Sunday, and my favorite uncle was going to be running one of his thoroughbreds, "Jerry Town Dave," at the Aqueduct Racetrack in the afternoon. As the newly arrived, almost favorite, nephew, it was very important for me to make an appearance, not to mention that I loved the horses and planned on making a sizable wager in support of my uncle.

That morning, we were all up early to get ready for the track, all, that is, except for Patty Ann; she overslept. The family left without us and told me to follow when my princess was ready. After several attempts, Patty finally woke up, but refused to leave until she put on her makeup (a two-hour affair...and it had to be perfect). Several hours later, we pulled up to the racetrack, and we were *so* late that the parking attendant didn't charge us. As we walked up to the entrance, they just waived us through. And as I looked up at the monitors, all I could hear was, "And it's Jerry Town Dave by five lengths."

My family can be a little tough on people they don't know, and they are definitely not known for their patience. *This was going to be a very...very... long four days.*

A Few of Our Regular Customers

Butcher Mike was in charge of the meat counter of the supermarket behind us. At the end of every day, he would come in for just one beer on his way home. He loved to bring a meat scale into the bar with him and bet other customers that they couldn't guess my weight within twenty pounds. I was 220 but in reasonably decent shape, and on a good day, the estimates ran from 180 to 200, and we would split the winnings. Mike, while swirling his one beer, would tell some of the greatest stories. He could take a simple, three-minute anecdote and drag it out for thirty minutes or more, while constantly swirling his "one" beer. *His timing was always impeccable.*

· · ·   · · ·   · · ·

John was my fast-talking car salesman from hell. On a good month, he would buy rounds of drinks for the bar and never left less than a 50 percent tip; on a bad month, I would have to carry a tab for him and sacrifice all of my tips. It worked out pretty well for me because John was top salesman at the dealership more often than not.

· · ·   · · ·   · · ·

Chris M. owned a car leasing company in Huntington Beach, but his true love was gambling, and he would bet on almost anything. Over the years, he became so good at it that he made it his profession, and as he developed his clientele, he would use the local restaurants as his "office."

Hof's was one of Chris's regular stops, and he would come by at least twice a week to meet with his clients. On one of his many visits, Chris asked the manager of the restaurant if he would consider giving his son, Tom, a job. And the timing was perfect, because one of their busboys had just been picked up by the immigration department and was sent back to Mexico. They needed to replace him immediately; Tom was able to start the next day.

Chris spent a lot of time here for several reasons. First, and most important, were his clients, but his ulterior motive was Molly. Molly worked as a cocktail server and Chris had spent the better part of a year trying to get close to her. This was one of those situations that was all about the ego. Chris was forty-nine years old and wanted her…badly. Molly was twenty-three years old and loved to tease him…she lived for it. Chris tried everything, offering dinner, drinks, taking her on vacations, to leasing her a car, but nothing worked.

A couple of weeks after starting his new job, Tom pulled his father aside and asked him for a couple of hundred bucks. When Chris asked him why, he told his dad that he wanted to join a few of the guys whom he worked with on a trip to Mexico for the weekend. Chris peeled off three $100 bills and told him to have fun...that is, until Chris found out that his son was going to be spending most of his time with Molly. Not only was Molly having one hell of a good time teasing Chris, now he was being asked to pay, so that his son could enjoy Molly's company. Chris was a little more than just pissed.

He called Molly over to the table and bluntly asked, "Okay, how much?" Molly's innocent reply of "For what?" didn't sit really well with an already angry Chris. "You know for what. I want you. How much?"

Molly just leaned across the table, giving Chris a great view of her cleavage, looked him straight in the eyes, and said, "You can't afford me."

Chris placed ten $100 bills on the table, but she just smiled and shook her head. Chris placed another ten $100 bills on the table. Her eyes got a little wider, but she still shook her head no. Another twenty $100 bills were placed on the table, but this time, Molly spent a little more time staring at the $4,000 Chris had just laid on the table (it was a lot of money...and after all, he really wasn't *that* bad). Chris noticed her hesitation and pounced. He put another $1,000 on the table.

This time, Molly looked up and said, "Okay, you win... I'll be off work in an hour."

Chris looked her straight in the face, picked up his $5,000, and said, "Fuck off. I just wanted to see if you had a price."

He was smart enough to understand that he wasn't going to get every woman he wanted, but he *did* expect a little respect. When Molly chose Tom for her date for the Mexico trip, it was more to screw with Chris than it was to spend time with a seventeen-year-old boy. Chris needed to make a point, and he did, *but he had to spend the next six months dealing with Molly's advances.*

• • •   • • •   • •   •

Trish, a waitress from a restaurant down the street, would stop by before every shift for a quick shot of tequila. She was tiny, but could outdrink any sailor I had ever met. She once talked me into trying a "Mexican Flag" before starting my own shift—Green Chartreuse, 151 Rum, and Grenadine, layered in a pony glass. Talk about being fast, two of those and my hands were flying, and so were the drinks. I got into the habit of having a couple of these cocktails before I would start my shift (just to get my heart pumping). That is, until *all* of my waitresses convinced me to stop drinking them. Yes, I was fast, very fast, but apparently, I was also *very, very* sloppy, and the girls got tired of cleaning up *my* mess.

Rita, who took it upon herself to keep my bar clean, would walk around picking up empty glasses and wiping down the bar every chance she got. All of the bartenders were in the habit of keeping a small glass against the entrance to the bar to act as a "doorstop," to keep it from being lifted too far back (if the glass was removed, the door would hit the glass shelves next to it).

Rita, lovely Rita, on one of her cleaning patrols, removed the glass that kept the entrance door to the sunken bar from hitting the shelves that held all of the glassware. Within a few minutes, "nature" was calling, and I rushed to get to a bathroom before anyone needed another drink. I lifted the door to get out from behind the bar...and the door hit the top shelf, which then hit the shelf under it, which then hit the shelf under that, and all three shelves landed on the last shelf holding the majority of the glasses.

They found me on my hands and knees under the remains of over five hundred cocktail glasses. Shattered glass was *everywhere* and it took over a week to clean it up.

A Few of My Friends

Tamara, Daniela, Sarah, and Jackie...there could not have been four women with more passion for life, and as luck would have it, all four were cocktail servers working at the same bar. Tamara is a tall, five-foot-eight brunette, with an athletic build and great tits. Daniela is only five-foot-two, but an exotic beauty that exuded pure sex. Sarah is blonde, petite, with a pair of legs and an ass to die for. And then there was Jackie, tall, with dirty blonde hair, perky breasts, and an attitude.

It was Friday and I had the night off. The five of us started drinking champagne at around five, and never slowed down. We blew right through happy hour, and with the band starting in about an hour, we began shooting shots of tequila. We were pretty drunk, having a ball, and getting *real* touchy-feely.

Daniela and Sarah were giving the "straight" girls in the club something to talk about, and I have no doubt that more than just a few of them were starting to doubt their sexual preferences. Jackie was busy flirting with several groups of guys at the neighboring tables when Tamara decided to find out if I was all talk.

She gracefully moved to me, leaned forward, and slowly, ever so slowly, started to nibble on my lower lip. Her tongue quickly darted out and caressed my own. In spite of the amount of alcohol I had already consumed, or maybe because of it, I started to respond. Our tongues moved together as one; our lips were perfect together...soft, light, sensuous. I felt that my heart would actually stop if she pulled away too soon. I was quickly losing myself in our building passion; our lips were the only point of contact in what was the most intense kiss of my life.

We were having a great time and had no idea how late it was getting until we heard the bartender call out, "Last call." And we were "hammered." There was absolutely no chance that any of us could drive home, *let alone find our cars*, so we stumbled across the parking lot to a local Embassy Suites hotel and I checked us all in. It took us about an hour to get our clothes off and fall into bed, not because we were having so much fun; we were just too damn drunk to function. We hadn't even noticed that Jackie had never made it to the room, but she enthusiastically filled in the blanks for us when we saw her again on the following Monday.

As I was busy checking us all into the hotel, Jackie had spotted a tall, good-looking "bad boy" in the hotel lobby. We all know the type…long, flowing hair, several large "tats" visible on his well-muscled arms, carrying his leather "biker" jacket—the type women seem to fall "head over heels" in love with. After a few short minutes of conversation, Jackie and her new friend left the lobby, climbed onto "bad boy's" Harley, and took off to Las Vegas. She barely made it back in time to start her Monday afternoon cocktail shift and fill us in on how great her weekend was.

They had stayed at a great hotel on the strip (but she couldn't remember the name). They gambled, and won, at a different casino (but she couldn't remember where). They were having an amazing time and felt that they had each found their soul mates. By Sunday afternoon, they were obviously in love, their relationship was perfect, and the sex was amazing. So what better way to end the weekend than to go back to the wedding chapel they just passed and "tie the knot"?

Jackie and her new "husband" were the perfect match for each other, with only one major problem. Jackie had been having such a great time with "bad boy" that she had totally forgotten that she was already married, and that her husband had been home, waiting to take her away for the weekend. Instead, he spent his weekend searching hospitals and police stations, looking for his missing wife. *Needless to say, both of her marriages were short lived.*

● ● ●   ●   ●   ●   ●   ●   ●

Pete was a bartender at a small restaurant a few minutes from Hof's, and I would try to stop by at least once a week for a "quick one" before starting my own shift. It was about three-thirty when I walked in and noticed that the only other customer in the bar was a very attractive, very drunk brunette.

She introduced herself as Lei Lani and apologized for not wearing anything but her workout clothes—skintight shorts and a workout bra, advertising her tight, washboard abs. A masseuse by trade, Lei Lani was trying to talk Pete into giving her a ride home so that she could get ready for her next appointment. Pete wasn't sure what to think, but Lei Lani kept drinking, and the drunker she got, the nastier she became. Even after Pete cut her off, she would lean over to take a sip of my drink, and tried even harder to convince Pete to take her home.

Pete's "little" head finally took over and he called Mark, the night bartender, to ask him if he would come in an hour early so that Pete could leave, and then he could "work out" with Lei Lani. Seconds after Mark came in to relieve him, Pete grabbed Lei Lani's car keys, took hold of her arm, and they took off in her Mercedes.

About twenty minutes passed, and neither Mark, the few customers in the bar, a couple of employees, nor me could wait any longer. Mark called Pete to see how his workout was going, but all Mark heard was an out-of-breath Pete, huffing and puffing, and was told that he would call back in a few minutes. A few minutes later, Pete called back, looking for a ride back to the bar. The very athletic, very physical, very drunk Lei Lani had pulled a knife on him and was chasing him down the block, *not exactly the workout Pete had in mind.*

A regular customer picked Pete up and brought him back to the bar just in time to hear Mark, on the phone, tell Lei Lani that he had no idea who she was talking about. Apparently, she remembered the bar, but totally forgot the name of the bartender who had taken her home.

• • •   • • •   • • •

As much as I loved and appreciated Joe P., Beth was the most important person in my life when it came to my new career; she was a better teacher and truly cared about our chosen profession. The single most important lesson of all was when she showed me that morally, ethically, and professionally, Kurt was an asshole, and what he had been teaching me was a huge mistake. He was gone a few weeks after I had started, when the general manager caught him stealing. I was never quite sure if Beth had anything to do with it or not, but I never forgot her training. Hof's Hut may not have been considered a *real* bartending job by some, but it was, without a doubt, the best thing that could have happened to me.

From the first day of my employment at the restaurant, I was treated like family. I will always be eternally grateful for the time and education that I received from everyone there. I arrived back in California with only one purpose: to become a "professional" bartender. And thanks to my very knowledgeable friends at Hof's Hut, I was well on my way to achieving my goal. The on-the-job training they forced me to go through was invaluable, and because of my Hof's "family," it was always a pleasure to start my shift; I had never considered it "work." That's why when our general manager, Burt, was told that he had to leave to open a new location across from the John Wayne Airport, I felt like someone had hit me with a bat. He was going to be taking a couple of key employees with him, and as a result, our family would be breaking up. It was time for me to make a change, and I was wondering, *would the last two years of bartending be able to qualify me to work in a real bar?*

As much as I didn't like what was happening, the timing was good. My friend Joe P. was working as the night bartender at Lorenzo's, a restaurant only a few minutes from my apartment, and they needed to replace their day bartender. Joe was able to land me the job without so much as an interview or resume. *Apparently, his recommendation was enough.*

*Jokes, use them wisely…and ethnic jokes **only** amuse the person telling them, never the ethnic group it's about.*

The delivery… It's all about the delivery, timing is everything
A few of the "one-liners":
"Did you hear about the Pollock who shot an arrow into the air? He missed."
"Polish martini? A marble in a glass of 7 Up."
"Did you hear about Manual Labor? The new president of Mexico?"
"Have you ever had rodeo sex?"

As you're making love to your wife, aggressive, hot, passionate, you're between her legs, pounding hard and furious, and as you lean closer to her, seconds away from completion, you call out your girlfriend's name, and she bucks until you're thrown off.

*A young professional had a little too much to drink last night. She woke up lying next to a very large elephant. "Damn," she proclaimed. "I must have been **tight** last night."*

The elephant glanced over and muttered, "Ah, not so much."

Lorenzo's

• • •   • • •   • • •

The entrance to the restaurant was a long, narrow corridor but soon opened up onto two distinct large rooms. The dining room was set up with large, cozy booths along three walls, with sixteen tables located in the main area. One wall of the room opened up to the lounge area, and the first thing you notice was a small stage and dance floor off to the right, and a sunken bar located in the back of the room. The dining room could comfortably seat eighty and the bar area another sixty, small by some standards, but we were always busy for lunch and dinner, and the lounge offered live entertainment five nights a week.

The actual bar was set up with two bartending stations and chairs for ten; it was small, but very functional. We had a great staff of servers on the floor with Joe P. behind the bar at night, while I was primarily working the day shift. We made a great team, and would often swap shifts to keep from getting bored. Joe P. was left-handed and his "well" setup was exactly the opposite of mine, as my "well" was set up for my right-handed pour. At the end of my day shift, I would quickly change the "well" to suit Joe P. and informed my bar patrons that it was time to "rape" the bar. It was our way of closing out all open bar tabs so that the night bartender didn't reap the benefits of the day bartender's work (we were friends, but our tips are our livelihood). As I mentioned, Joe P. and I worked well together. Our personalities, skills, and work ethic were similar, and after all, he was my mentor. We were both fast. I was *very* fast, and young enough to think that speed was important, while Joe P. was "only as fast as he had to be." *Obviously, I still had a lot to learn.*

• • •   • • •   • • •

Joe was about to escalate my training. He had a very good understanding of the skills I had been able to learn while at Hof's, but now I needed to learn *his* way. As the day bartender, I was now responsible for the bar's cleanliness, the cutting of all the fruit required for the garnish of each drink, and the preparation for all bar mixes. We made all of them using formulas that Joe P. had created. The Bloody Mary mix, margarita mix, even some of the martinis were all premade before I started my shift.

At the end of my shift, I was also responsible for restocking the bar and making sure Joe's "well" was set up and ready to go the moment he stepped behind the bar. As I mentioned, I was right-handed, he was a lefty, and all of the bottles of liquor in the well had to be in the right place for each of us. At first, I thought it a bit much, but then I realized that Joe P. did the same by restocking and setting up for me when he ended his shift. When I came in, in the morning, *my bar* was fully stocked and ready to go.

A part of my escalated training with Joe was our pride in the bar, keeping it neat and clean. Once a week, every Saturday morning, Joe and I would ask one of our busboys to come in and help clean the bar, on our dime. Management was too cheap, so Joe and I took it upon ourselves to pay them, and it was worth every penny. When we started the week, our bar was spotless, every liquor bottle was wiped down and lined up, with the labels facing front; all the glasses sitting on the back bar were cleaned and polished, the stainless steel sinks and refrigeration were scrubbed cleaned, and everything was in its right place. Even the wooden slats that we worked on were taken outside and steam cleaned.

It was Joe's wish, as well as my own, that I become a "professional bartender," not just someone going to school or killing time until he figured out what his real career was going to be. Joe, and his peer group, the "professional bartenders" in the area, needed me to step it up a notch, quickly...*so that I would fit in.*

• • •   • • •   • • •

We started calling it a "speed run" when a few of us got together to drink—a lot. There would be only three, maybe four, of us, but never more. From the moment we would finish our shifts, we would start to pound down the cocktails, usually closing the bar that we would have started in. At two in the morning, we would head over to a local twenty-four-hour bowling alley to keep the party going (we always carried a flask of what we were drinking in our bowling bags, along with the ball and shoes, of course). We would stay there, drinking and throwing bowling balls down the alley every few minutes, until one of our favorite little "dive bars" opened at six in the morning. By lunchtime, we would have hit at least four of our little gems and just be getting our second wind. We wouldn't stop for anything—no food, no rest, just non-stop drinking in as many bars as we could stumble into.

This would continue for at least two, but usually three, days, and our employers all knew that even if they could find us, we would be in no condition to work. We weren't completely oblivious to our surroundings, which was why there were never more than four of us on any speed run; we needed to make sure that there were enough of our friends left sober to cover our shifts. We didn't want to lose our jobs. We just needed to escape reality for a little while…and although our employers might have been a little upset, and maybe a little jealous, they all understood.

•   •   •   •   •   •   •   •   •

Topper, the self-proclaimed king of rock and roll (second only to Elvis), whether playing for five or five hundred, he played his heart out. He was an awesome entertainer, and his following *was* impressive. He played at Lorenzo's every Tuesday through Saturday night and had been filling the lounge with his loyal following for years.

Even after he left, Joe P., our friend Jimmy, and I remained part of his faithful following. Regardless of what club he played in, we always made it one of our destinations. We would promote him every chance we got, and in return, he would promote us…*it always helped when the featured entertainer supported the antics of single bartenders looking for a little action.*

Many, many years later, the investment firm I was working for held a seminar at a hotel in the area. After the meeting, several of us, including my boss, went into the lounge for a drink. As we entered the lounge, I looked toward the stage to see my old friend, Topper. He returned my gaze and immediately called out, "Giuseppe Antonio Pietro Palmese, how the hell have you been?"

All I could do was smile, and try to convince my employer and the prospective clients with us that I hadn't seen Topper in many years, and that I really wasn't a regular customer there.

•   •   •   •   •   •   •   •   •

I was single…and playing hard. My day shift was treating me well, I was making good money, and I had my nights and weekends open to have some fun. My reputation as a bartender worth visiting was growing among the other bartenders in the area, and as a result, I was also expected to visit them as well. I started sending flowers, every week, to the female bartenders who I became acquainted with, usually to say thank you for "taking care of me" when I would visit their clubs, but also as an opportunity to generate a little romantic interest. I had developed an affinity for beautiful women in the industry. We kept the same hours, we had lots of fun, and we *always* had something to talk about. As I had mentioned, I was playing *hard*—and my florist bill was *huge*.

• • •   • • •   • • •

A friend of mine told me about a little, isolated town along the coast of California called Santa Cruz. It was a college town, with four all-female colleges in the immediate area; there was also one coed college, but that didn't concern me much. I'm only one man…*and besides*, there would be *hundreds* of single women to choose from.

I was fortunate in that I did not have to work on New Year's Eve (a request I made the day I was hired). I hated it, both as a bartender *and* as a customer. There were just too many amateur drinkers on the streets to suit my taste. You know the type. They get to go out maybe once a year, drink as much as they can, as fast as they can, to celebrate surviving the past year, and hoping that next year will be better. They are usually rude, inconsiderate people who can't handle their liquor. *I wanted no part of it.*

I thought it *the* excellent opportunity to check out Santa Cruz. I left a little before midnight. I wanted to be on the road, many miles away from the drunks, as the New Year came in. I entered the city limits at around six in the morning and checked in to a motel on the beach. A little breakfast, a nap, and I was ready to check out the local clubs. A twenty-five-year-old, single bartender in the middle of hundreds of lonely female college students… *It became an annual trip of mine for the next four years.*

• • •   • • •   • • •

I was passing the afternoon at a local establishment, enjoying a very meaningless conversation with the bartender, Claire, when one of her servers joined us after her shift was over.

Jasmine was young, slim, kind of attractive, with long, brown hair and beautiful brown eyes; she had an exotic but innocent look about her. Or so I thought, until she proclaimed, "I'm going to have some great sex tonight."

And I asked, "Does your current boy toy know what to expect when you get home?"

"Not really," she said, "but I sure do hope he can slap me around a little." *So much for innocence.*

The next hour was spent in a very open conversation between Jasmine, Claire, and I. Jasmine was so confused; she couldn't understand why a man would want to "go down" on a woman. "Doesn't it taste funny? Doesn't it smell? And foreplay is so overrated. I just want to 'get right to it.' And by the way, a man's dick doesn't have to be any more than this…" She held up two, very tiny fingers. "How could any of this result in great sex?"

I took it upon myself to try to educate this poor lost girl and show her the error of her ways. Not that I'm any expert, but I have had one or two opportunities to please women. First and foremost in my mind is always oral sex. The soft, sensuous folds of a woman's vagina, the "scent" of a woman, unique and totally arousing, and the subtle fragrance can denote a woman's *level* of excitement. The involuntary twitch as the tip of my tongue caresses each fold as I get closer to her clitoris. There is nothing, nothing more exciting to me than to have the woman I'm with convulsing in the throes of an orgasm that is the result of my head between her legs—*nothing*.

Foreplay…I can spend weeks on this, but six to eight hours is usually enough. The scene is set, the candles are lit (but not too many), with the right series of tunes playing in the background (having sex in time to the music can take the actual act to a whole new level—soft, "romantic" music is not always appropriate). A fireplace, a good bottle of wine, and hours spent discovering each other; then a shower, a massage…an entire evening could pass before we actually "get right to it."

The "slap" she was hoping for was not one of my favorite things to do when I'm with a woman, but there have been moments…and timing is everything. An occasional, unexpected, "forceful" caress, with proper timing, can transport you from a "making love" scenario to a gut-wrenching, hard core, intense sexual experience, combined with some serious, multiple orgasms. The added benefit of being with a woman who enjoys a relationship a little more physical are the "toys" that seem to go with the experience (nipple handcuffs were always one of my friend's favorites).

The only comment made by Jasmine that I was forced to agree with was about size, and that a man does not have to be big to satisfy a woman. According to the comments I've overheard while behind the bar, usually, by the "size challenged" among us, *it is not the size of the ship that matters; it's the motion of the ocean.*

Please, if it's a battleship coupled with the ocean's motion? Then that two-fingered canoe crap will never feel the same.

A Few of Our Regular Customers
Hack and Doreen owned the liquor store next to the restaurant and shared our parking lot. It was very convenient for them, as they were always my first customers of the day. I would leave the side door open for them so that they could come over for a "morning pick-me-up" before we officially opened.

They were a lovely couple, and over the years, we became good friends. I would often start my day, or end it, depending on how late I was out the night before, with a cup of coffee with Hack. He would open his liquor store at six in the morning and have coffee ready for all of his friends and regulars.

Every so often, their daughter, Sharyl, would join them for an early dinner. It was obvious from the very first moment that I was introduced to her that she was *way* out of my league. She was twenty-seven years old, attractive, always impeccably dressed, and she wanted nothing to do with me; *she obviously had great taste.*

Someday, somewhere, maybe in a couple of years, she might give me more than just the time of day... I was hoping.

•   •   •   •   •   •   •   •

Curt and Jean made it a habit to stop by every Monday afternoon at around two. It was the slowest part of my day and I would normally use that time to clean my back bar. I would first pull all of the liquor bottles from the shelves, wipe down the shelves, and then polish the bottles as I put them back in their place. It was also the perfect time to "sample" the liquors that the majority of my customers would never ask for. As creatures of habit, most of my customers rarely sampled something new, but Curt and Jean were exceptions, and we tried *everything*, at least once. It was during one of my "cleaning" sessions that we developed an appreciation for Amaretto and Frangelico, realized that Crown Royal was a bourbon that a scotch drinker could handle, and that Green Chartreuse should be banned from the planet.

A Few of My Friends

Over a period of about two years, Jimmy C., Joe P., and I were inseparable. The three of us had become members of what *we* considered as an "elite group of bartenders" whose reputations seemed to be far more impressive than our actual lives. There were about a dozen of us in this group, all very competent, all very professional, all very honest, and all of us in high demand by the club owners (when needed, any one of us could be called upon to cover a shift in any one of a dozen dance clubs or restaurants in the area). I was still very young, and the only reason I was even considered a part of this group was because of the accolades, support, and training given me by my mentor, Joe P.

Every Saturday night, the three of us would pile into Joe P.'s Pantera (the nicest car between us) and make an appearance at any one of these clubs. Jimmy (being the approximate size of *one* of my legs) would always be riding the center console. As members of this self-proclaimed "elite group," we were *always* considered "invited guests" of the owners. Our cars were parked in front of the club by the valets. We never waited in line or paid to get in. And we never, ever, paid for a drink. *Obviously, the decision to become a professional bartender was the right one…not even the actual club owners were treated this well.*

• • •   • • •   • • •

Ken was a character, about five feet five inches tall, one hundred fifty pounds soaking wet, with scraggly brown hair and a very short clipped, graying mustache. Although he always avoided the question, I guessed him to be about seventy years old. He had decided to open a little neighborhood bar across the street from my apartment. He called it his retirement. My friend Jimmy was his night bartender and I tried to visit both of them at least twice a week.

When Ken wasn't in his bar, he was watching the quarter horses at the Los Alamitos racetrack. In the truest sense of the word, he was considered a "handicapper," with much of his time spent researching and analyzing *everything*. The racing forms, the "expert" predictions, the jockeys, the trainers, the horses, the weather conditions, past post positions, previous results, their times, *everything*. For a professional, horse racing was just like the stock market, with education and proper research; you took the "gambling" part out of the equation and increased your odds of picking winners.

While I was growing up, my dad would take me with him to watch thoroughbred racing at Belmont, in New York, and as I watched Ken working his calculations, he very much reminded me of my dad. He used to do the same thing. I enjoyed Ken a lot, and when he asked me to join him at the track, I jumped at the chance.

We arrived at the track at eleven in the morning for lunch. It gave Ken several hours to do his homework and put the finishing touches on his research. By the time the first race was scheduled to go off, he had chosen his picks for all nine races. Even though I was still young and relatively innocent, I correctly assumed that Ken knew far more about this than I did, and I mirrored every bet that he made. Every once in a while, I would throw in a long shot, but I always bet on Ken's picks, in addition to my own.

The day was sunny and warm, with just a slight cooling breeze. It was *perfect*. There were nine races scheduled, and by the end of the day, Ken and I had won all nine races, *perfect*. We left the track feeling so good about our fortunes that we decided to try our luck again on the following day.

As we did the day before, we arrived by eleven and our routine was essentially the same. After Ken completed his "homework" and picked the horses he liked for all nine races, we settled in for some serious drinking. The day before, Ken had been focusing on the horses and didn't want alcohol to interfere with his choices, but today was different. His research for today was done, and we felt the need to celebrate our past success. Just like the day before, the weather was perfect, and so were we. Nine races, and once again, nine winners—*perfect*.

With our current success, there was no way we could *not* make it three in a row, and we weren't willing to change *anything*. So once again, we arrived at the track by eleven. The day was perfect, the homework was done, the research was extensive, and the first race went off by two. By the end of the day, as Ken and I heard the announcer say that there was a photo finish to decide the winner of the ninth and final race, we just nodded our heads in disbelief. The first eight races had been business as usual for us, and it really didn't matter to us which horse won the last race. *Between us, we had picked both horses.*

As we drove back to Ken's bar, the realization hit that in three days and twenty-seven races, including the "dead heat" we experienced in the last race, Ken and I had picked *twenty-eight* winners.

Instead of sitting back and enjoying our success, as Ken had decided to do, I, in my infinite wisdom, determined that Las Vegas needed a visit. After all, with my current track record, *how could I possibly lose?*

The next twenty-four hours were fast and furious, but the only thing worth remembering was the flight there and back. The casinos I visited were now the proud recipients of every penny of what I had won during the last three days, and then some. *Now, talk about a perfect ending.*

• • •   • • •   • • •

Every once in a while, one of our bartender friends would slip up. This time, it was Jack's turn. He was a friend who worked as the night bartender at a club just a block from Lorenzo's. He was also considered to be a member of our self-proclaimed "elite" group. He is married to a very lovely woman by the name of Clair, who is *also* a bartender, and truth be known, she was so much better than Jack. Jack might have been a member of our group, but Clair got all our action. They *seemed* to have had the perfect relationship, that is, until the day Jack made the front page of the local newspaper.

It was a beautiful, sunny afternoon, and Jack was driving Harbor Boulevard, just past Disneyland, when he spotted an attractive woman trying to hitch a ride. He immediately pulled over and engaged her in conversation. In less time than it took to turn off his car engine, three cop cars pulled up and surrounded him. The lovely woman looking for a ride turned out to be an undercover cop, and it became obvious, very quickly, that Jack chose the wrong time to offer her money for her "services."

It was a sting operation, complete with photo journalists from the local newspapers, and there was Jack, sitting in his car, smiling up at the photographer.

It made the front page, and needless to say, *Clair was more than a little upset*. The second phone call Jack made after his arrest was to me, to make sure I included Clair on my weekly distribution of flowers…*his obscure way of making an apology*. Clair *loved* the flowers, and *our* friendship remained good. Unfortunately, *Jack wasn't so lucky*.

• • •   • • •   • • •

It was a very lazy Sunday, my day off, and I was bored. I had completed all of my necessary chores—dry cleaning, laundry, basic food shopping—when I noticed a little "hole in the wall" beer bar that demanded my attention.

For a Sunday afternoon, the place was packed, and as I entered the room, I was greeted with a very long, thirty-stool bar off to the left, and nothing else…just the bar. I sat at the only empty stool I could find and ordered a beer. As I made myself comfortable, I realized why the place was so busy. The bartender, Beth, was pretty, but it wasn't her cute body, long, flowing auburn hair, or the lively, perky, bouncing breasts under her blouse that kept her customers there. It was her personality, that attitude that I'm so fond of. Exciting, bubbly, sparkling…words aren't enough. She simply "lit up" the room.

I finished my first beer, ordered my second, and enjoyed the show. As I finished, I laid a twenty on the bar for Beth and got up to leave. She looked at the twenty, and me, and told me that it was too much. "No, it's not. You're great," I said. "I really enjoyed the show."

She picked up the money and came around the bar, took hold of my arm, and escorted me to the really busy section of the bar. She informed a very large gentleman that he had to move, and without question, he surrendered his bar stool to me. Beth placed the twenty, and a new beer, in front of me, and softly proclaimed, "*This* is the twenty-dollar seat." She had placed me on the section of the bar that was directly in front of the bar sinks. As I made myself comfortable, Beth went back behind the bar to wash glasses.

As she leaned forward to put her hands in the water, she smiled. I leaned forward to get a better view. The front of her blouse had moved away from her body, allowing a perfect view of those very lively breasts. As she vigorously washed the glasses, her breasts seemed to have a life of their own. And as I pressed even closer, I was only inches away from them.

She could definitely light up the room—and the "twenty-dollar seat" lit me up. After another beer, and a few more twenties, I slowly eased my way out, called my florist, and added Beth to my weekly florist delivery.

• • •   • • •   • • •

When Jack gave me a call, he had only spent one night in jail for the pandering charge and was back to work the next day. His boss had just hired a new bartender for the day shift, a real "hottie," but I didn't give it much thought because I don't usually appeal to "hotties." That was always my friend Joe's role.

I attempted to walk into Jack's club at around four the next day and found it almost impossible to squeeze in. It was still a little early for a "happy hour" crowd, but it was already two deep at the bar and getting busier. As I literally squeezed into the room, I noticed the owner standing in a quiet corner, and I slowly worked my way next to him. As we exchanged greetings, we both settled in to watch the hottie, Jeannie, work the room.

She looked amazing, and Jeannie was "working" every guy at the bar, and they were *all* guys. She was good behind the bar. She was a good mechanic; the drinks were made quickly, efficiently, with no wasted moves, but these guys were obviously not there for the drinks.

Jeannie was wearing a very short skirt, one that barely covered her butt, and a cotton "tube top" that struggled to contain her very large breasts. Her bare midriff was "tight" and the size of her nipples, without the benefit of a bra, made it damn near impossible to concentrate.

It was a small bar, with all the backup liquor located on the shelves above the bar. Jeannie was constantly climbing up to reach for the extra bottles, which, of course, was the only reason to be standing at the bar. As she stretched and climbed, every part of her body strained against the brief material she was almost wearing. The perfect "V" formed by two beautifully proportioned legs would be at eye level as she reached up, her breasts would jiggle uncontrollably when she dropped back down, and through all of it, she showed *zero* emotion.

No one seemed to care that she was essentially brain dead. The task of making change was beyond her, and her conversation was nonexistent. She was putting on a great show, and it was now three deep in the bar.

I leaned over and mentioned to the owner, "You know, if someone were to ask her what her name was, she would probably have to check her driver's license to get the answer. Who's watching the money?"

He whispered, "No worries. That's what I have **him** for." And he pointed to the little Mexican bar back standing next to the register.

Whatever Jeannie didn't do, Juan did. He was her backup; he collected all the money, restocked the bar as needed, and kept the bar clean. All Jeannie had to do was stand there and pour drinks. Juan went totally unnoticed. All eyes stayed riveted on Jeannie's every move. *Did I mention that it was now four deep at the bar?*

Men are pigs! And, yes, she was also added to my weekly florist delivery, even though, in the months that followed, we were never introduced, and

I'm pretty sure she had no clue who I was. As I mentioned, I was *never* considered "hottie" material.

• • •   • • •   • • •

My friend Annie was just another reminder for me that I didn't appeal to hotties. She was an up and coming designer but was working as a cocktail server to pay the bills. I would stop by and visit often, in the hopes that I could convince her how good we would be together. I have a spot on the end of the bar that I love, and in addition to the unobstructed view of the entire bar, it's close enough to the bartender's well so that I can watch and *learn* from my friends working the bar, as well as allow me to be next to the server's station as they work their shift. *It's the only time I can flirt with Annie.*

Annie has a real attitude that I truly love, and a confidence issue that I was trying to work on. In her mind, she thought she wasn't *that* attractive, had a little bit of a weight problem, and blamed that for her lack of a current boyfriend. I was speechless, which didn't happen too often, because in my mind, she was freakin' amazing. Simply put, Annie was gorgeous. She could walk into a room and the room would light up. I had a hard time *not* thinking of her physically, but her face is what I fell in love with. She walked into the bar to start her shift, looked up and made eye contact, she would smile, *and I would melt.*

Jeannie wasn't the first and I'm pretty sure that Annie won't be the last, and as all great wingman do, you learn to cope and accept rejection. Annie is a very intelligent woman and she knew how easy it would be for her to *have me*. Even after offering her breakfast, to spend some time together, to take her shoe shopping, to help her with some business opportunities, to be used and abused as her personal sex slave, all I got was *the smile. I can live that.*

• • •   • • •   • • •

My friend Matt was tending bar at a very successful disco and lounge, just a few minutes from the entrance to Disneyland. It had also been my first stop, years earlier, when Joe welcomed me back to California.

Matt was always trying to come up with a new idea to keep his regular customers coming back for more, and this time, it was pure genius. Our bar patrons always seemed happiest when given an opportunity to celebrate *something*. A round of shots, a toast, and a race to see who could finish it first would always put people in a better mood. Matt created his "special shot," a little sweet and sour mix, with a float of vodka, for sixty cents.

It was a Tuesday night. It was early. The bar was full, but boring, when Matt decided to shake things up. He placed one of his "special shots" in front of everyone on the bar, about twenty people, and proclaimed, "First one is on me, but after this, the shots will cost you sixty cents."

Everyone lifted their shot glasses, Matt's toast of "To Tuesday," and the race was on to see who could finish his shot and slam the glass to the bar first. Not a minute later, one of the patrons ordered another round of "specials" (about $12), then the race, and that was how it started. They would literally pour thousands of these every night. They were priced right, everyone *loved* the ongoing celebration, and no one *ever* got drunk. *Matt had calculated that one bottle of vodka could make as many as one hundred of his "special shots."*

●　●　●　　●　●　●　　　●　●　　　●

I was having a pretty good time working with my friend Joe, but when my girlfriend Patty Ann told me that her dad was considering buying a couple of beer bars and would like to talk to me about a possible partnership, I jumped at the chance.

The Bartender walked up to Jon, a customer sitting at the bar, and noticed that he had a little man sitting on his left shoulder, about twelve inches tall. He ordered a beer for himself and a shot of bourbon for the little man. The little man jumped down, drank the shot, and walked down the length of the bar, kicking over every drink he passed. A few minutes later, he jumped back to Jon's shoulder.

A few minutes later, Jon ordered another shot and a beer, and once again, the little man jumped down, drank the shot, and continued down the bar, kicking over any other drinks sitting there...then back again.

Bartender, curious as hell, walked over and asked Jon, "What's up?"

Jon looked up with a very dejected look on his face. "I was walking along the beach a couple of weeks ago when I came across a fancy bottle lying in the sand. I picked it up, but as I was rubbing the sand off it, a genie appeared. He looked down at me and said, 'Your lucky day, I'll grant you one wish, but one wish only.' I asked for a twelve-inch prick, and he nodded to his left."

The Pubs

• • •　　• • •　　• • •

As beer bars go, they were beautiful. It was a concept created by a local restaurant entrepreneur. They were built in anticipation of acquiring full liquor licenses for each location, for their eventual conversion from beer bar to nightclub. As you enter, the custom made oak bar was to your left, with twelve bar stools and a waitress station in the middle of it. There were a half dozen tables set up for the customers, but the room was dominated by three pool tables, each one in its own semiprivate area. The back kitchen area was set up for the eventual addition of the kitchen appliances, and there was a walk-in cooler, large enough to handle one hundred kegs of beer.

From their onset, both locations were set up for the eventual conversion to English pubs, but the liquor licenses never came through. The current owner was already operating three successful restaurants and had no interest in keeping two beer bars.

The days prior to opening were spent cleaning. Although the actual design of the bars was appealing, the exiting staff was pretty upset that the previous owner hadn't made good on his promises. They gave up caring, and by the time we took them over, the pubs were a mess. They were just beer bars, but that was no reason for them to be dirty. Nothing turns off a potential customer faster.

• • •　　• • •　　• • •

It had been only a couple of months, but the combination of keeping the bars clean and employing competent, attractive bartenders was working; we were growing the business. My first two hires for the bartender/manager positions had been Kathy and Carolyn.

Kathy was coming from a background of six years as a cocktail server, but had never been behind the bar before. She had been working with me at Lorenzo's when I offered her the management position for the Anaheim location. Kathy wasn't sure she could handle the change financially, but when she realized that *all* of her current clientele would follow her to the pub, she accepted. Every morning, before she would start her shift, she would literally cover her head and slip into the back office before anyone could see her, then she would spend thirty minutes applying her makeup, and by the time she made her entrance at the start of her shift, it was perfect; *everyone* appreciated the effort.

•   •   •   •   •   •   •   •   •

Carolyn was cute, with short, brown hair and large, round eyes. She was also the proud owner of one of the first "boob" jobs in the county. I would love to be able to call it "breast enhancement surgery," but it wasn't. They were hard silicone implants that looked as uncomfortable as they felt.

Carolyn was an extremely hardworking employee and would do anything asked of her...anything. There was one major flaw to her character; she seemed to fall in love a lot. After breakfast one morning, and a very long cup of coffee at a local shop, I found out that she had been previously married— *nine times...she was only twenty-nine years old.*

About three months after our opening, Carolyn had started her shift in a mental mess; she was a nice person, almost too nice, but when it came to her relationships, she just didn't understand that love and sex were two entirely different emotions. In her mind, you had to be in love with the person you were having sex with. Sex for the sake of just sex just didn't make any sense to her. She had spent the previous evening having sex with one of her new "friends," and when he left in the morning, she was told that "no, he didn't love her."

I did what any good manager would do. I took her into my office and let her cry. I made myself available, but when she finally settled down, things started to change. She started to nuzzle the base of my neck, and as she offered her lips to mine, I responded. She slowly lowered herself to her knees in front of me, but as she unzipped my pants, I stopped her and pulled her up. It just wasn't right for her to service me when *she* was the one who needed the support. I needed to be taking care of her, to be there for her, not the other way around. As she was standing against the wall of my office, I lowered myself and gently removed her panties from under her dress. Ever so softly, I started to kiss the folds of her vagina, my tongue darting out every few minutes to keep her interested. I was there for a very long time. *I truly do love the taste of a woman in the morning.*

When Carolyn's orgasms hit, they hit hard and lasted for several minutes. It took her a while to come back to me, and as the waves of pleasure subsided, I gently pulled her panties back up and left her to compose herself. For the rest of the day, she just smiled. It wasn't until the following weekend that I realized the mistake I had made. *Carolyn was in love again, but this time, with me.*

I wasn't willing to lose a good manager because of what I had let happen between us. We were both consenting adults, but I did take advantage of the situation and I now had to fix it. I took my time and worked very hard at making sure Carolyn knew that our daily interaction and the flirtations between us were just that. We were friends, not "lovers."

A few months later, she "hooked up" with one of our regular customers, and after a couple of weeks and a quick trip to Vegas, she had husband number ten. Apparently, she had decided that her tenth wedding would be an excellent thirtieth birthday present to herself, and of course, *he loved her.*

. . .   .

We didn't have a full kitchen in either location, so I kept the lunch menu simple but creative, offering some of my mom's "special recipes" that I would cook at home and bring into the bars. For our Friday night "gift" to the happy hour crowd, I would have a dozen pizzas delivered from a restaurant across the street and pass them around the bar. Word got out very quickly that we offered "free" food during our Friday afternoon happy hour, and it wasn't long before we were standing room only. (The pizza cost $80, but it helped sell an extra five kegs of beer every Friday.) Within a few months, between both locations, we served more draft beer in Orange County than any other establishment.

Operating a beer bar when you don't necessarily like beer is a little tough. Sure, beer is okay with pizza, or watching football, but for me, that was it. So on one busy afternoon, when I decided to buy a round for the bar, I did not expect them, nor did I want them to reciprocate, but they did; the whole bar bought back and that was when my problems really started. When I took over the pubs, I could handle one, maybe two, beers at a time, but no more than that. By the end of the first year, I was up to a case of beer a day. For those of you who aren't aware of the effects, a case of beer a day equates to about twenty extra pounds, all in the gut. So much for all that physical training that used to be such a big part of my life. About the only exercise I was getting these days were the "arm curls" with one beer in each hand.

When I was operating the two pubs, I was on the road. I would open the Anaheim location at eleven in the morning and would work through the lunch rush with Kathy. I would leave after lunch and arrive at the Santa Ana location in time to work through the happy hour rush, change the shift, and then head back to the Anaheim location. I would stay there until we closed it, and then I would leave for Santa Ana to finish the night—six days a week. I can honestly say that on many of those nights, the only reason that I'm still alive is because of the "speed bumps" located between the lanes of the freeways. For the most part, I was either too tired or too drunk to see, and bouncing between the speed bumps kept me in a relatively straight line.

•   •   •   •   •   •   •   •   •

Nancy only worked weekends, nowhere near enough hours to justify the damage she caused. Her boyfriend, from the island of Hawaii, caught her cheating on him, and the day he found out, he came charging into the pub to confront her. One look at his face and she started screaming for help, and unfortunately, she got it. The few customers in the bar all stood up to help protect my poor, innocent bartender. If they had only known how foolish that was… Her boyfriend was large and loved pain, which became obvious when the first of my loyal customers punched him in the face and he just smiled. In the next thirty minutes, every table and chair in the place was broken, and every customer in the place was either gone or also broken, and Nancy wound up with a broken arm. I arrived just as the cops were taking the boyfriend out in handcuffs and Nancy was waiting for a ride to take her to the hospital.

The next weekend, I was covering one of Nancy's shifts when my sympathy for her very quickly turned into rage. My inventory numbers were off, and from the looks of my initial investigation, my lovely Nancy was, in fact, cheating…with my wine salesman. She was having sex with the salesman to get the wine for the bar "off invoice." She was then selling the wine during her weekend shift, and was putting the money in her pocket. I fired her for stealing the minute I got confirmation from the salesman; he was really worried about losing his job as well.

About a month later, I received paperwork from the Employment Development Department for Nancy's unemployment insurance. Not only was she responsible for the damage done to my bar and the actual loss of the cash that she stole from the wine sales, now she was going to collect unemployment as a parting bonus. She had been one expensive bitch.

•   •   •   •   •   •   •   •   •

As engagements go, mine and Patty Ann's was a joke. She was beautiful and intelligent, but we just never "clicked" as a couple. I spent most of my time operating the bars, and she would rarely visit, and our sex life was more of an accommodation, not an attraction.

After one of our infrequent interludes, she started telling me how grateful I should be. After all, *she* just *saved* me $2,000. When I asked her how she was able to accomplish this from my bed, she got up and walked over to the closet.

Still naked, she pulled out a floor-length Russian Sable fur coat and put it on. As she started to model this sacrilege to animal rights, she shared with me how it was listed for $4,500, but she was able to buy it on sale for just $2,500. *In her mind, she just saved me $2,000.*

I rolled out of bed and gave her a quick peck on the cheek for being so thoughtful and caring. It wasn't until I informed her that "I" was able to save $4,500 because *she* was going to return it immediately. *That's when the realization hit me that my fiancée was one self-centered, crazy bitch.* We never really formally ended our engagement, primarily because I was still her father's partner, but our sex life ended that day.

• • • • • • • • •

The Libation Station was located across the street from Disneyland, and was *the* hangout for all of the bartenders, waitresses, and bar owners in the area. As you entered through the front doors, you notice that it was, in fact, *all* bar. A very large, square bar situated in the middle of the room, and that was it. No tables or chairs anywhere, just the bar, and a small stage in the corner of the room. The bartender working the day shift was "Pepsi," tall, dark, and handsome, as the old cliché goes. He was also a true bartender's bartender, with a great sense of humor, excellent bartending skills, and good bar presence, but it was his sarcasm that everyone remembered most. He would always wear what had become the bartending uniform for the area, a white shirt with black vest and tie. The vest was made by a local seamstress, always black, with two gold chains across the front, and her family crest over the left pocket. Every bartender in Orange County owned at least one of these.

I had a few minutes to kill before I had to change the shift at the Anaheim pub, so I stopped by the "Station" for a real drink. The bar was full, all twenty-four barstools, and everyone a bartender or waitress whom I had come to know. So I did what any professional would do to make a good impression: I bought a round of drinks for the bar, and a few minutes later, the bar bought back, all twenty-four of them.

Pepsi put up a sixteen-ounce mixing glass in front of me, picked up a bottle of Chivas Regal (my drink of choice at the time), and started to pour. He just held the bottle upright, and every four seconds, he would announce, "This one's from Pete...and this one's from John...and this one's from

Scott…" This went on until the first mixing glass was full. He put a second one in front of me and kept pouring. "This one's from Betty…this one's from Pat…this one's from Dean…" And so on. As the second glass was topped off, Pepsi put a third mixing glass in front of me, opened a fresh bottle of Chivas, and kept pouring; he still had a third of the bar to go. "This one's from Patrick…and this one's from Don…and this one's from Cathy…" Until he finished the order. The last sixteen-ounce glass was almost full when I heard, "And this one's from me." Pepsi bought the last drink, put *one* ice cube in the last glass, and pushed it toward me. "Here you go, Hotshot. Have some fun." *It took me almost three days to finish the damn thing.*

I had been out of the bar business for about five years when my wife and I decided to drive out to Palm Springs for dinner (a two-hour drive from the Libation Station). It was a normal, hot evening, typical for the Palm Springs area, *only* about ninety degrees. I left the jacket of the three-piece suit that I was wearing in the car and walked into the restaurant in just my white shirt, dark vest, and tie. My wife and I sat at the bar while we were waiting for our table to be ready, and I looked up to see a familiar face. Pepsi hadn't changed a bit. Always the professional bartender, he was still wearing a white shirt, black vest, and tie. I wasn't sure that he had recognized me, but after he placed our drinks in front of us, he stood there, polishing a wine glass, and asked, "So, Joe, what bar are you working at these days?"

It was as if I had never left the business. He saw a white shirt, black vest, and tie, and in his eyes, I was still a bartender.

• • •   • • •   • • •

Tina was a moment in my life that will never be forgotten. The first time I saw her, I knew I was in love. Five feet six and three quarter inches of perfection, she was wearing tight-fitting shorts and a halter top that didn't quite cover her midriff, and of what I could see, her body was flawless. I first saw her as she was moving into the apartment across from mine. As she was struggling to unpack her car, I walked over, introduced myself, and picked up a couple of the heavier boxes. The apartment she was moving into was already furnished, and she only had a few items to carry in, so in less than twenty minutes, we were done. She had just arrived from some place up north and was hoping to find work in the morning. "Up north" was a little vague, but I was so happy to be in the same room with her that it really didn't matter where the hell she came from. I lingered as long as small talk permitted, but I had to get ready for work, so as I was leaving, I told her where the pub was and invited her over for a beer after she finished unpacking.

It was approximately eight o'clock when Tina walked into the bar, and my heart almost stopped. I thought she looked perfect when I first met her, but that was before she took the time to put on her makeup and pour into the tightest pair of jeans imaginable. She had on four-inch heels and her long, blond hair was pulled back away from her face. She wasn't wearing a bra and her small, very erect "headlights" were pointing directly at my heart.

We sat for hours, drinking beer and talking about anything and everything. By the end of the night, I asked her if she would consider working with me at the pub I had two locations and could really use the help. Of course, it didn't hurt that during the course of the entire evening, every pair of eyes in the bar was staring at her. She would definitely be able to increase my business. She needed to find a job as soon as possible and I needed to have the new love of my life close to me, so it was perfect when she accepted my offer.

It didn't matter that she had never worked in a bar before. I would teach her. It didn't matter that I had no idea where she came from or who she really was. She would tell me eventually. *And* it didn't matter that I was engaged to my partner's daughter. I would figure that out later. I decided that we should car pool on her first day on the job; after all, she would need to stay close to me during her *training*. Talk about using my "little head" to think with instead of my "big head."

In the morning, I walked over to Tina's apartment to see if she was ready for her first day. The note on the door told me to come in and make myself comfortable. As I entered the living room, music was coming from the bedroom and I could hear the sounds of the shower running in the background. The bedroom door was open, and from where I was standing, I had a perfect view of Tina, in the shower. My heart was racing and I wasn't quite sure what to do. *Should I move into the kitchen area, as a true gentleman would, where the view wasn't as impressive? Or should I stay where I was and enjoy the moment?*

Her hands were slowly moving along her perfectly proportioned body, and as I was about to leave, she glanced up and caught me staring. I was embarrassed, and very excited, but just as I was about to turn away, Tina opened the shower door and nodded her approval. The only thing that surprised me about the next few seconds was that I actually took the time to get out of my clothes before joining her.

Once in, I lowered myself to my knees and gently caressed her labia with long strokes of my tongue, and within minutes, in spite of the hot water flowing over our bodies, she started to shiver. And as I applied a little more pressure, she came. Using just my tongue, I slowly worked my way past her navel until I reached her breasts, concentrating first on her left nipple, then her right. I so truly enjoyed the way that she tasted. I started to lower myself down again, but instead, I cradled her butt in my hands to lift her up so that her legs draped over my shoulders. Tina was bracing herself, using the top railings of the shower stall, and as my tongue found its way back along the folds of her vagina, she came again. She smiled down at me and we decided to take it out to the bed. Needless to say, she was a little late for her first day on the job, but by the end of that day, she received a raise and was promoted to assistant manager. *That damn "little head" of mine.*

• • •   • • •   • • •

We were entering the start of the holiday season and my parents were driving out from New York to spend Thanksgiving with me, and the new love of my life. I only had a one-bedroom place, so I gave it up for my folks (just another excuse to spend more time with Tina). I was trying hard, maybe a little too hard, to make a good impression for my folks. I made reservations at Lorenzo's for Thanksgiving dinner for the four of us; it would be a good chance for them to meet Joe P. and they wouldn't have to spend all day in my tiny kitchen cooking. It was a great dinner. Joe P. was perfect, as always, and the management and staff made my folks feel like royalty. Unfortunately, we had to make it an early evening because they were leaving the next day and wanted to get an early start for their return trip to New York. My dad dropped us off at the apartment and left, saying that he had to pick up a few things for tomorrow. And after I said good night, I went over to Tina's apartment.

Very early in the morning, I walked over to my apartment. My mom and dad were already up, the car was packed, and they were ready to leave. My mother brought me into the kitchen to show me what my father had accomplished. I was in shock. My refrigerator was packed with food. In the top section, there was turkey, turkey salad for sandwiches, turkey soup, mash potatoes and gravy, lots of it; in the freezer section, there was extra turkey stock, turkey, and turkey meatballs. They had decided that it just didn't feel like Thanksgiving unless they cooked, so my dad went food shopping after he had dropped us off at the apartment, and he and my mom spent the entire night cooking a twenty-pound turkey with all the trimmings. As I walked them out to their car, my mom pulled me aside and said, "Son, when you told me how much in love you were, I was very upset. But now that I've met her, I'm okay. She's gorgeous, but she won't last. We'll call you as soon as we get back home. Love you."

Within days of my parents leaving, Tina and I started to drift apart. She was in my life for only another four weeks, two as my employee and two as my neighbor. She started going out with Mike, a regular customer from the bar, and eventually moved in with him. It seemed that his engine shop was more successful than my bars. *Moms are always right.*

It was only a matter of time, but a few weeks later, Mike mentioned that he came home from work one day to an empty apartment. Tina had disappeared, along with *everything* that he owned. She had cleaned him out, from furniture to all of his clothes. She hadn't even left him his toothbrush.

· · · · · · · · ·

I was having some engine work done on my '74 Corvette when Mike offered his services at his engine shop. After spending several weeks telling me how good he was, and that his past relationship with my ex-girlfriend wouldn't be an issue, I let him have some fun. The result was a "balanced and blueprinted" engine, and a promise that it would be very, very fast. In my mind, it meant that I would get to my weekend destination that much quicker. I picked up the car late in the day and headed north. It was a routine that I have developed over the last couple of years. My destination, Santa Cruz, was a favorite little college town of mine and I wanted to be miles north of Los Angeles before the New Year's Eve drunks headed home.

The car was performing magnificently, and I was cruising at about a hundred miles an hour when I saw the flashing lights of the highway patrol car behind me. I immediately pulled over and stepped out of the car to wait for him to pull up behind me.

As he walked up to me, I tried to have this really innocent look on my face, and said, "I'm sorry, Officer. I have no idea how fast I was going."

As he started writing my ticket, he looked over and said, "Well, I was doing a steady seventy-five…and you were steadily pulling away from me."

I quickly shut up and considered myself lucky. Anything over seventy-five in this state and he would have locked me up. *This was only a ticket.* Back on the road, I watched as the officer turned around and headed back, and I floored it, now cruising at about a hundred and twenty. What sense does it make to have a balanced and blueprinted engine if I couldn't drive it? And besides, I didn't want to be late for my college girls. It was three in the morning, New Year's Day, in the middle of nowhere, when it happened. The technical term was that I "blew a rod." The reality was that my hotshot mechanic wasn't as good as he thought he was, and it took almost twelve hours to get the car towed back to his shop.

I wouldn't be able to prove it, but maybe it was his way of getting back at me for introducing him to Tina. I never did make it back to Santa Cruz.

· · · · · · · · ·

It was two in the morning and I had survived a very intense competition between myself and the night bartender of the Libation Station. It was tequila, and I matched him shot for shot. It had been a very quiet evening and I had closed the Anaheim pub location at ten and then wandered into the Station, looking for some company and a nightcap before heading home. The rest of the evening quickly became a blur as the two of us powered down shots until we closed the bar at two. We both stumbled to our cars, and as I was just a short distance from my pub *and* my apartment, I chose to drive.

I was weaving only "slightly" and was just passing eighty when I heard the sirens behind me (I hadn't been on the road for more than five minutes). The flashing lights from two police cruisers had apparently gone unnoticed by me, but the sirens definitely got my attention.

This was a time before Mothers Against Drunk Drivers (MADD), and the term driving under the influence (DUI) hadn't been coined yet. It was different back then, when having "one too many" didn't *seem* to have quite the impact as it does today, and our city's finest weren't held responsible and accountable for all the stupid things *we* do.

The two policemen carefully approached me, and as I rolled down my window, I had to think fast. I proclaimed, "Officer, thank God. I know I was going a little fast, but the alarm went off in my bar a few minutes ago and I really can't afford to have some lowlife rob my place of business. Can you help?"

Now, there was no doubt in my mind that as soon as I rolled down my window, the officers could smell the tequila. I simply reeked of it. They had pulled me over on what was normally a very busy street, but at two in the morning, on a Monday night, it was just the three of us. The two officers looked around at the empty street, looked at each other with a smile on their respective faces, and told me to follow them and try to keep up. A few seconds later, they took off, heading toward my bar, their lights flashing and sirens blaring.

As I pulled up in front of the entrance, they already had their guns drawn and told me to unlock the door. *I mean, it wasn't as if I actually had anything to really worry about.* By the time they finished their inspection, I had locked the door behind us, turned on the lights, and we finished their shift drinking beer and shooting pool.

A Few of Our Regular Customers

Deputy Johnnie D. was a homicide detective with the Santa Ana Police Department. A soft-spoken, very large man, he was six feet five inches tall and weighed north of 300 pounds. Deputy Johnnie would stop by a couple of times every week for a quick game of pool with my bar manager, Carolyn, and a cup of coffee. He never drank alcohol.

My bartender and I had just finished restocking the bar, in anticipation of a busy happy hour, when we heard the roar of motorcycles pulling up in front of the bar. Minutes later, one of our newly arrived guests rode his Harley directly into the bar, and as his friends followed him in, I realized that I was going to need a little help. These gentlemen were not regulars of ours and had already started to manhandle the ladies in my bar. I picked up the phone and called Johnnie D., and within minutes (what seemed like hours at the time), we heard the police sirens. I glanced out of the front door to see the results of my phone call—six motorcycle cops, followed by several patrol cars, pulling into my parking lot. As the police entered the bar, the "club" members lined up on one side of the room, with the cops along the opposite side. The police outnumbered the "club" members, **and** they had guns, but I was still worried. Deputy Johnnie stepped up and, in a very soft, controlled voice, took control of the situation. Every club member was personally escorted out of the front door, and to add insult to injury, the six motorcycle officers continued the escort to the city limits. From that moment on, for as long as I owned the pub, the officers and their families had an open invitation to be my "guests" every Sunday afternoon.

• • •　• • •　• • •

Our law students, our children, our future—okay, enough of that. Tweed's pub Anaheim was almost a block away from a very successful law school, and during most of the year, their students would use my off-campus location for some very selective studying. The official end of their school year was marked by the unofficial "law school marathon." During the week of their final exams, the student who finished the exam first would leave the steps of the law library carrying an empty beer pitcher, then run the block to the back door of the pub to have it filled up with the beer of his choice. Final exam week would increase my beer sales by at least ten extra kegs. *I am always in support of higher education.*

• • •　• • •　• • •

The word "dapper" comes to mind when trying to describe Joshua, a very black, very Jamaican gentleman. He had a clean, crisp accent, and I could always count on him to fall in love with whomever I chose to put behind the bar. I was in the market for a new car and spent most of the afternoon trying to decide…a black Lincoln Continental Mark IV with black interior or a white Lincoln Continental Mark IV with white interior, and then I saw it, in the middle of the showroom floor. It was pink; it was the only word that I could use to describe it. The salesman called it "light red," but it was definitely pink. It was also gorgeous, with lots of chrome and a white interior, but it *was* pink. About an hour after seeing it, I drove the pink Lincoln right off the showroom floor, and as I pulled it in front of the Santa Ana pub, Joshua was standing outside. As I said, he was Jamaican, with one hell of an accent; he took one look at my new pink car and proclaimed, "Mudda Pucka, I got three black chicks keep that car so cleeeeeeean."

I was floored. Here he was, my little dapper gentleman, speaking "ghetto" English, and, in fact, was actually born and raised in Santa Ana, CA. *And*, as I was about to find out, was one of our local colorful pimps. *He **loved** my new car.*

A Few of My Friends

"Lying Joe P." I was sitting in a friend's restaurant with a couple of the regular customers, enjoying Joe behind the bar (a rare daytime occurrence). It was a quiet, lazy day, with nothing going on that generated any *real* excitement. Pat, a quiet, nervous little man, was sitting next to me. He was always so worried that his wife was going to catch him doing something wrong, and, if truth be known, he *never* did anything wrong. He was "henpecked" and Joe P. was bored.

Pat was getting a little jittery about picking his wife up from work by five (he just couldn't be late). He looked over at Joe and asked him what time it was, and without so much of a glance, was calmly told that it was four-forty-five. Pat freaked. His wife was going to kill him if she had to wait. He threw some money on the bar and ran out. About ten minutes later, Joe received a phone call from one very pissed-off patron. "You piece of shit! You son of a bitch! Goddamn you." Pat was sitting at a red light and glanced down at the clock on his dash: three-thirty. A straight-faced Joe P. is so damn convincing that most people would *never* question what he said, *but you definitely need to look out when he's bored.*

• • •   • •   • •   •

"Lying Joe P." Again. We were spending our Sunday afternoon at the most popular "pickup" place in Newport Beach, The Red Onion, and as usual, Joe P. was on his game, and I was whatever he needed me to be. This time around, standing there in his cowboy boots and Stetson hat, it wasn't that hard to convince anyone that he owned a couple of cattle ranches in the southern part of Texas. Joe introduced me as the owner of a chain of steak houses and the primary buyer of his beef.

He was on a mission: to talk to and convince as many women as possible to give him their phone number. The promise of a future relationship with a cattle baron was just one of the "carrots" he dangled in front of them. In the next three hours, he convinced twenty women to hand over their phone numbers. He was getting so good at this that he didn't have the need to write *anything* down. He committed *every* name and number to memory. *Not one of the twenty women expecting his call received one. For Joe, it was all about the chase.*

. . . .

The bars were doing well, but my relationship with Patty Ann was pretty much nonexistent. Her father had lost patience with me as soon as he realized that being his son-in-law was no longer an option—and that greatly affected our ability to work together in the operation of the bars. It was also becoming more obvious that she had a plan for her future, and I wasn't going to be *a* part of it. So it was no surprise to anyone when we formally dissolved our partnership. We sold the more successful Anaheim location and Patricia was given the Santa Ana location by her dad.

A few minutes after leaving the meeting with my now ex-partners, a Cadillac swerved across two lanes, jumped the center divider, and hit my beautiful, pink "pimpmobile" head on. After the insurance company totaled the car, they sent me what they thought it had been worth, and I took the money and called my friend Jimmy C. *I needed a little vacation.*

. . . .

Several years later, I stopped by the Santa Ana pub for a couple of drinks with an old friend of mine. It had been almost ten years, but there was Patty Ann, still behind the bar. She hadn't changed much—still attractive, a little older, and, hopefully, a little wiser. Without saying a word, she took our drink order and placed the two beers in front of us. I had changed since I last saw her. I no longer had curly hair or the mustache that I had been so proud of, but I would have thought that she would still have remembered me. I was talking to my friend, as all Italians talk, with my hands, when I knocked over the beer in front of me. I hadn't taken a sip yet. Patty came over, wiped up my mess, and placed another beer in front of me. She still hadn't said a word to me and I still hadn't taken a sip yet, when it happened again. Patty Ann walked over, placed my third beer in front of me, and shook her head, then said, "You never did know how to fucking drink."

A few minutes later, Patty Ann's son came running into the bar to say good-bye to mommy. When I looked up, I saw a familiar face, Joshua's, the boy's dad...*so much for being a little wiser.*

Kelly walked into his favorite Irish pub a bloody mess. As he stumbled up to the bar, the bartender, O'Hara, looked up and asked, "What in God's name happened to you?"

"It was Mr. O'Shaunessy, it was," Kelly replied. "I saw him coming, a two by four in his hands and the look of the devil in his eyes."

*"Kelly, I **know** you. You **saw** him coming, and you never go into a fight empty-handed. What did you have in your hands?"*

"O'Hara, my Lad, it was Mrs. O'Shaunessy's left breast…a fine, magnificent thing that it was, but not much good in a fight."

The Marlin Club

. . .   .

Catalina Island is twenty-seven miles off the coast of California. The island, for the most part, is considered a wildlife refuge and game reserve, and it was not uncommon to travel through the interior to check out the herd of buffalo. The town of Avalon is approximately one square mile and located on the southeastern corner of the island. It has fourteen bars and restaurants within a three-block radius, and except for the occasional visit to one of the local gift shops, there wasn't much else to do on the island except drink. (I had been told that there was also a nine-hole golf course, but no one I ever came across with could ever remember playing it.)

I was going to stay with one of my closest friends, Jimmy C. Jimmy was slight of build, looking a little like "Howdy Doody" from the children's show of the '60s. In addition to being one of the best bartenders in the county, he was also one of the funniest. I spent the last several years supplementing my bartending knowledge with the pearls of wisdom and attitude that Jimmy was thoughtful enough to share with me.

I flew in to Avalon Harbor in one of the oldest sea planes still allowed in the air; it had seen service during World War II and had a terrible time staying afloat. It was my first trip to the island, and although flying for me had never been a problem, the water seeping into the flight cabin when we landed rattled me more than just a little. Apparently, it was normal because the other six passengers just lifted their feet to keep them dry as the pilot maneuvered the plane to the ramp for unloading.

Jimmy met me at the "airport" and showed me to his apartment, a one-room affair, with a bathroom, a small kitchenette, and a queen-sized bed, nothing else. The apartment was only half a block from Jimmy's work, the

Marlin Club, a local establishment with red swinging doors at the entrance and a bar that was patterned in the shape of a boat. There were twenty-two stools around the bar and it had two pool tables, one located in the front as you walk in and the other in a small back room. The brass plaques on the bar gave notice to the time and effort that the regular clientele spent there. There was one that stood out more than the others, Gene "back in ten minutes" Smith. Gene owned the gift shop around the corner and would open his shop at eight in the morning, and by eight-ten, he would put a sign on the door, "Back in ten minutes," and walk into the Marlin Club. He would start his day with vodka and orange juice, then vodka seven, vodka water, and by the end the day, vodka rocks—all day long, from eight-ten in the morning until he closed his shop at six at night, six days a week.

Jimmy started his shift at six and introduced me to the owners, Barry and Patricia. Pat would work the early morning shift from six to ten, Barry the day shift from ten to six, and Jimmy from six at night to closing. As Jimmy started his shift, Barry took it upon himself to show me the night life of Avalon. That first night in Avalon, Barry bought me drinks in thirteen of the fourteen local establishments, while sharing with me how he bought the bar using the proceeds of his fishing boat. It wasn't until much later that I found out that he bought the fishing boat from the proceeds of bringing illegal aliens across the border in the trunk of his Lincoln Continental. *The stories this man shared while behind the bar could have filled a book.*

By the time we got back to the Marlin Club, Jimmy was just closing up, so Barry locked the doors and poured us another drink. Barry and Pat lived above the bar, Jimmy lived half a block away, and we were on an island. *How much trouble could we get into?*

At six in the morning, the front door opened and in walked Patricia to start her shift. She was only five foot four inches tall, and some might say that she was a little heavy (but never to her face). Personally, I thought she was perfect. The look on her face when she saw the three of us still drinking at six in the morning was one for the books. Barry stood six feet four inches, weighed in at around 250 pounds, and that one look from Pat was enough for him to run, not walk, to their apartment upstairs. I wasn't sure what to expect, but Jimmy didn't have to be in to start his shift for another twelve hours, more than enough time for him to sleep it off and get ready, and I was just a *guest* passing through.

Patricia walked behind the bar, poured herself a gin and tonic, refilled our drinks, and off we went. As the day passed, Barry had passed out and didn't show up to cover his shift. Patricia was on a roll and kept pouring us drinks, but Jimmy started to coast a little so that he could cover his night shift. Although nothing was actually said, this must have been Pat's way of putting

Barry in his place, because when her shift was over, she took it upon herself to also show me the night life of Avalon. This time, we hit all fourteen of the local establishments, and by the end of the evening, I was done. I woke up on one of the pool tables and Jimmy was on the other…welcome to Catalina Island. *I was still waiting for the "sun" part of my weekend.*

My last day on the island was quiet, comfortable, and extremely educational. It was a Monday morning, and Barry and Pat decided to take Jimmy and me to Lani's Pancake Cottage for breakfast. Lani's was three doors down from the Marlin Club, and by seven in the morning, there was a line a block long, waiting to get in for the finest breakfast on the island. Lani was a very large, intimidating, caring woman—a legitimate Hawaiian princess from Maui—and her husband, Frank, was the chef. When I was introduced to her, she immediately came over and gave me a *huge* bear hug. Now, I am not a small man, but when she put her arms around me, I was lost, suffocating between two very large breasts.

The actual breakfast lived up to the hype—it was great. As we were finished and the empty plates were being removed, Patricia made me an offer. Jimmy had been working for them for almost three years and had a really bad case of *island fever*. The man with the great, funny disposition had become a cranky asshole, and he needed a change. Patricia also thought it a good idea, and having *already* checked with my current employer, she decided that I would be a better choice than any of the bartenders currently living on the island. Barry thought I would make a good choice because he liked the way I tipped. *I had been set up.*

They had it all worked out. Jimmy and I would swap jobs *and* apartments. I had replaced Jimmy at the restaurant I was working at in Orange County several years earlier, and they had already talked to my boss. Jimmy would get his old job back and move into my apartment. I would take over Jimmy's job at the Marlin Club and move into his apartment.

Barry and Pat offered me $36 a shift, a pretty good wage, considering that the average for bartenders at the time was only $28, and an additional fifty cents an hour bonus for every hour I worked, if I made it through the season, and they would pick up my rent. My mind was still trying to get a handle on what I had just been offered when I noticed that Pat had asked Lani to join us. Frank and Lani were in the process of opening a Lani's Pancake Cottage in Maui. It was under construction and was scheduled to open the following year. If I showed them that I had the ability to work on an island during the coming season, then they would be prepared to offer me their bartending job for the winter season on Maui.

Five months working on Catalina Island with two weeks' paid vacation, a bonus, and my rent paid by Barry and Pat. Six months working on Maui with two weeks' paid vacation and all of my room and board paid by Lani and Frank. A single bartender being paid to live in paradise, I didn't need much time to say yes. I went back to the mainland, spent a week "pub crawling" to say good-bye to my friends, sold my two cars, packed my bags, and was back on the island in time for the start of the season, Memorial Day weekend.

• • • • • • • • •

First impressions are so important, and so hard to repair. I had arrived on the island a little early to get accustomed to my new surroundings. I was about to start my first shift at the Marlin Club and I thought I had dressed appropriately—clean white shirt, black bartending vest, and diamonds everywhere. I had a diamond necklace with a matching diamond pinky ring on one hand, and a ring, with the initials JP, in diamonds, on the other. It took only fifteen minutes for me to realize my *huge* mistake. The next day, I deposited *all* of my jewelry in a safe deposit box at the local bank, but I spent the next two years with the label "Diamond Joe" thrown at me every time a local customer thought I was making more money than he was. "Why tip? He doesn't need the money. Did you see those damn diamonds?"

• • • • • • • • •

In spite of the "Diamond Joe" incident, the next several weeks went well. I had settled in quite nicely. I had decided to get in shape while on the island, so I watched my diet and stopped drinking. Working seven days a week at the Marlin Club made it pretty easy—sleep until noon, wake up to a late breakfast at Lani's, and then get ready for work; nice, comfortable, profitable, but pretty damn boring. Some of the locals decided to "set me up" with the new girl in town (apparently, she would be just perfect for me).

Cindy had moved to Catalina a week earlier and was a nurse at the local hospital. Our mutual friends brought her into the club to introduce us. Her blond hair was cut very short and she was all of five feet tall…and then there were her eyes. A man could lose his soul staring into those eyes.

It had been quite a while since I spent any time with a woman. I had stayed away from the tourists and was trying to focus on making money and getting into shape. It wasn't that hard to understand that after our first meeting, I couldn't get her out of my mind. I sent her a dozen roses the next day, and the week after, and the week after that. She was always polite and thanked me, but she wasn't ready to date anyone just yet. I thought I had been doing pretty well to this point, but I was feeling just a little lonely, more than just a little horny, and wasn't willing to give up so easily. I mixed up the varieties, but I made sure she received flowers every Monday, along with a dinner or breakfast invitation.

During this time, I started to get a little creative with our tourist trade. I had "Ski Catalina" T-shirts made with a picture of snow skiers on the front, and passed them around for all the bartenders on the island to wear. This is Southern California; it doesn't ever snow here on the island. In the long run, it probably helped out the island economy because we had several tourists make reservations for our holiday snow season. Then there were the tourists who I had convinced that the island was in a separate time zone from the rest of the country—and, yes, effective just two months ago, we were now accepting US currency. When I got really bored, and to break up the busy season, I would start rumors about myself, just to see how long it would take to get back to me. The rumors were usually about flying to Vegas and either hitting a very large jackpot or coming back married, but always about something ridiculous, and never true. When you live on an island, you'll see that people will look for anything to break up the boredom, and it never took more than two days for the stories to get back to me.

As the season continued, the flowers continued, and Cindy seemed to be getting more comfortable with my advances. When she heard about some of the things I was doing to "assist" with our tourist trade, she started to open up to me. She finally accepted one of my dinner invitations, but only if we could leave the island. She didn't want us to be one of those rumors that I was so proud of starting. I thought it would be an excellent idea and called my friend Jimmy. He was still living in my old apartment on the mainland and he had kept the spare bedroom available for guests.

I planned our date to include quarter horse racing at the Los Alamitos racetrack in Orange County and dinner at a friend's restaurant. It had been six months from the first moment I met her, and the hope that I could make a good enough impression for her to spend the night with me physically and sexually pleasing her was almost too much to bear.

The following Sunday morning, we left the island on one of those leaking World War II vintage sea planes and landed in the San Pedro Harbor. When I first decided to move to the island, I purchased a beat-up 1968 Oldsmobile for $200 and kept it in the parking lot next to the sea plane landing. It was a transportation car, one that I would only need to use about once every couple of months. I would need to jump-start it and fill the radiator with water *every* time I needed to use it, but it was paid for and it served its purpose.

Our conversation during the flight was pretty limited, and I was starting to feel a little nervous. After we landed and I jump-started the car, we left the San Pedro terminal on our way to the racetrack. Still pretty quiet, I was astounded when Cindy leaned over to my side of the car, unzipped my pants, and proceeded to give me one of the most intense, totally unexpected blow jobs of my young, innocent life. It was a forty-minute drive to Los Alamitos, and Cindy's lips were very busy. I came twice during that forty-minute drive, and I was *so* confused. I would never have imagined that I would get this kind of attention from a woman who took almost six months to accept a dinner invitation. I guess her "dry" spell had been even longer than my own.

We spent the next four hours drinking, talking, and gambling on the quarter horses, but I couldn't tell you if we had any winners or not; I was still in shock. As the ninth race was about to start, we left, so that we could check in with Jimmy before he left for work. Once again, as we pulled out of the parking lot, Cindy was back at it. I was just finishing my third orgasm of the day when we pulled up to my old apartment. I desperately needed some time to recuperate, so I left Cindy to get ready for dinner while I confirmed our reservations. I also wanted to make sure that the flowers I had ordered were waiting for us at the table.

Dinner was great, the flowers thoughtful, the bottle of wine, excellent, but we rushed through it and ended up at the apartment for "dessert" in record time. As I followed her into the bedroom, I was amazed at just how well she moved. I was naked, hard, and ready before she completed the distance between the door and the bed—all of four feet. I dropped to my knees in front of her and slowly started to remove her pants, when she suddenly grabbed my hands. I had no idea what to expect, or if I had done anything wrong, but she wouldn't let me continue. I was still on my knees in front of her when she told me that I needed to know a little more about her before she would allow me to see her naked.

What the...? Now, I have a fairly creative imagination and the thoughts running through my mind were driving me crazy. Why the oral sex so freely and easily given? My mind was racing, my heart pounding, panic was starting to set in as I expected the worst. As I sat back, she ever so slowly finished what I had started. I was mesmerized as her pants slid down those perfectly proportioned legs. She was about to lower the French-cut lace underwear when I heard the words "large tattoo." Here I was, with my mind and body going through my own private hell, and she was worried about a damn tattoo.

Now, that being said, *it was a very large tat...*an intricate, delicate black rose, covering the entire right cheek of her perfectly formed ass. The words "Property of" were stenciled in the middle of the rose, but the name of the person she had belonged to had been surgically removed. I listened intently as she spoke of her past life and how, at a very young age, she had become a member of a well-known motorcycle gang. She escaped from them about a year ago and thought that Catalina Island was the perfect hiding place to get her life back in order. Catalina had no highways, very few cars, and no motorcycles; her past wouldn't be able to track her twenty-seven miles across the sea.

As she paused, my initial panic subsided, and I slowly started to caress her soft inner thighs. We kissed long, slow, sensuous kisses. We played. We fondled. Then a massage, then a shower, then back. I couldn't keep my hands or mouth off her. We never did get to sleep that night and barely got out of bed in time to catch our flight back to the island. *It was one of the most amazing nights of my life...*

We arrived back in Avalon by eight-thirty, and by the start of her workday, she received another three dozen roses. For the next week, I had flowers delivered every day and I saw her every night. Maybe it was the result of the six months of anticipation...or maybe I just overdid it, but Cindy left the island the following week. Apparently, she wasn't interested in having "Joseph P." tattooed under "Property of" so soon after our first and only real date. *I still miss her and think of her often.*

•   •   •   •   •   •   •   •   •

Labor Day weekend is the unofficial end of the summer season and the weather was just starting to cool. Catalina is great this time of year. During the summer months, it averages ten degrees cooler than the mainland, and in the winter, it's usually ten degrees warmer. The weekends still get hit heavily by the tourist trade, but the weekdays are relatively calm. I have the perfect job; the Marlin Club is one of only two bars on the island that are open seven days a week, all year long. During the "off season," the rest of the bars and restaurants only open on the weekends. Monday through Friday, my regular clientele are the out-of-work bartenders and waitresses on the island... *It's a tough job, I know, but somebody had to do it.*

After a busy season, three months of working seven days a week with no days off, we were all ready for a little R&R (rest and recreation); for Barry, Pat and I, that meant Vegas. The three of us were pretty burned out and we really weren't too concerned about throwing a closed sign on the front door without any notice. Our regular customers, the islanders, would understand. I broke out the diamonds and some cash I had stashed in my safe deposit box and Barry made the reservations. It was a quick flight on the seaplane to Long Beach Airport (twenty minutes), and then a short hop to Las Vegas on a twenty-seat jet, operated by Scenic Airways. Scenic Airways would hold their flight for us until our flight landed from Catalina. We were in Las Vegas in less than an hour, from curb to casino.

First, the three of us went for three days, then back to Catalina for the weekend tourist trade. Then it was Barry and Pat for a day the following week, and then I would go for two days, then they would go back for another two days, then back for the weekend. Over the next several weeks, we made six trips to the city of lights and you would have thought that we would have gotten it out of our system.

Less than a week later, Patricia was sitting in the bar, sipping a gin and tonic, bitching about being back on the island. Island fever is the result of living and working on a small island, twenty-four/seven, without any opportunity to escape. You feel like you're suffocating and you become very angry, with everybody *and* everything. Patricia had reached that point, and the six previous trips to Vegas only seemed to make it worse. There was a gin tournament scheduled in Las Vegas that week and Pat was going to attend, with or without Barry. Reservations were made and *they* were leaving within the hour. I was going to stay on the island to get some work done, but then I would fly out to join them in a couple of days. We had our annual the Marlin Club party to plan for, scheduled for October, and we needed to spend some time on the island in preparation.

I arrived the following Thursday evening, and as I entered the lobby of the Sands Hotel, the gentleman behind the counter looked up and smiled, saying, "Good evening, Mr. Palmese. Does the casino know you're in yet?" Now, I'm a professional bartender, nothing more, nothing less. The casino shouldn't even know my name, let alone care whether I'm in or not. I quickly checked in to the room, made sure I had my diamonds on, and, with cash in hand, I walked down to the casino floor.

As I entered, I noticed that there was a small opening at one of the crap tables, and I decided to see if anybody else knew my name. The gentleman to my right had just lost the dice. He requested a "marker" for $10,000 then looked at me, my jewelry, my clothes, my attitude, and he decided to put it all on the line in anticipation of my first roll. I held the dice for a few moments, getting the feel of the table, and let loose, a three, craps. As the dealers cleaned off all the bets, my neighbor looked me over once more, the diamond rings, the attitude, and just motioned to the pit boss. Another $10,000 was placed in front of him, and once again, he put it all on the line. Without saying a word, I leaned over, picked up the dice, and rolled them down the table—a twelve, boxcars, craps, any name you use, the result was the same: my neighbor was out *another* $10,000. He glanced over and mumbled, "You didn't look like a fucking loser."

I quietly lowered my head, passed the dice, and went looking for a bartender to help relieve my embarrassment and pain.

After more than just a couple of scotch rocks (Chivas Regal was still my preferred choice), I started to feel just a little better about myself and decided to have dinner in the restaurant just off the casino area. I had eaten there several times and the cute little redhead working that night was someone I enjoyed flirting with over the last several visits. After dinner, she came by and asked if I had any plans for the weekend. I told her that I was flying home in the morning, and she just looked at me incredulously and said, "You don't live here?" That was it, I was done. The entire evening gave credence to the fact that I was spending entirely too much time in Las Vegas. It really *was* time for me to go home.

· · ·   · · ·   · · ·

The Marlin Club party is an annual event that everyone, tourists and islanders alike, look forward to with great anticipation. Barry was considered an old school bartender, a professional with good looks and personality. He felt that the owner of a bar, any bar, should not be the recipient of gratuities. During the time he spent behind the bar, any tips offered to him would be tossed onto the canvas awning above the bar. Twice a year, he would collect the money and use it to throw a year-end party to "celebrate" all of the Marlin Club regulars. He started this the year when he and Pat bought the bar, and in the three years since, it had become *the* party of the year. My first season with them had also been their busiest. Barry was forced to clear the canvas four times and the final count was a little over $4,000.

We scheduled the event for the last weekend in October and started to get ready. Only one problem: the Marlin Club could hold fifty on a good day, and we were expecting over 200. To make it simple, beer, wine, or hard alcohol would all be at a cost of $1 each. With $4,000 to work with, we were worried that the party might last the whole weekend...*silly us.*

When the day arrived, we covered the pool tables, took out all the bar stools and chairs, and overstocked the bar. We were opening the doors at noon, and with Barry and Pat playing the role of gracious hosts, I was going to be alone behind the bar.

They started pushing into the bar at exactly twelve o'clock, and never stopped. My friend Cathy and her longshoreman husband, Jack, were the first to arrive at the party. They were regular customers of ours who tried to visit the island at least twice a month, and they were always fun. Cathy was cute and one of the most flirtatious women I'd ever met, and Jack was big, very big, and I worked very hard at keeping him happy and not being one of Cathy's targets. It was getting busier by the minute and there seemed to be no end to the number of people pushing into the bar. As the party grew, Cathy made it her personal mission to make sure I was adequately compensated for working my ass off. With Jack's permission, she started selling kisses, $1 for a peck, $10 for full mouth, $20 for full contact...and every penny made its way to my tip jar. *She must have really liked me.*

As we got closer to six o'clock, the party was winding down, and I was finally able to take a little break. We had passed the $4,000 limit and began ushering our guests to the front door. I was exhausted. In the six hours we were open, I had served approximately 400 guests and 4,000 drinks (twenty-seven cases of beer, nine cases of wine, and forty-two bottles of liquor). It was fast, furious, *and the most fun I ever had behind the bar.*

Cathy came behind the bar and pressed against me. I could see Jack getting a little jealous from the corner of me eye, but I was too tired to care. I found out later that night that Cathy enjoyed flirting with me a little too much and Jack had made it abundantly clear that *I* was the *only* one who Cathy wasn't allowed to kiss. As she slowly pulled away from me, I noticed Jack putting three large ice buckets on the bar, filled with the results of Cathy's efforts. I had calculated that I had already earned about $800 on my own, but thanks to her, I had another $1,800. Dinner that night was going to be on me.

• • •   • • •   • • •

During the slower "off season," the tourists are treated better, the islanders have more fun, and there is a tendency to enjoy life with a lot less pressure. It was January and most of us living on the island during this time of year would often start our days early. We would enjoy a cup of coffee while sitting on the seawall overlooking Avalon Harbor. It is a beautiful sight and it has been said that if you sit there for about thirty minutes, *everyone* working in town that day will pass by you.

It was during one of those beautiful mornings when we saw three bikini-clad women on their way to breakfast. As they passed me, the tallest of the three looked over and asked which restaurant I would recommend, and without a second thought, Lani's Pancake Cottage was the first thing out of my mouth. I was still sitting there about an hour later when they passed by again; only this time, they went directly to the sandy stretch of beach in front of me to set up their blankets. (It must have been their way of saying thank you for recommending Lani's.) I was starting to stare and thought it best to leave before I embarrassed myself...the girls looked great and were making one hell of an impression.

Working in one of the only bars that stayed open during the winter months, it was only a matter of time before the girls found themselves in my bar. They had finished dinner at the Galleon, a local favorite for both dinner and live entertainment, when they decided to see what the Marlin Club had to offer. They recognized me from this morning and were very appreciative of my choice of restaurants.

They were on a mission, and we had pool tables and a full bar of lonely men. When twenty men fight to buy three beautiful women drinks, it's an event, even more so when these same three know how to work the room, shoot pool, and are looking for some action. They were wearing very light, revealing summer dresses and looked simply delicious.

Whether it was when one of them leaned over the pool table to take a shot or they would simply be sitting on one of the bar stools, all eyes were on them. Maybe it was the amount of alcohol everyone drank, maybe it was just trying to impress the women with their gallantry, but the girls couldn't seem to lose. By the end of the evening, they had outdrank, outshot, and outtalked the entire bar (except me, of course; I had become their hardworking, very attentive servant for the evening).

I had already given "last call" and was just starting to clean the bar when I realized that it was just the San Francisco Three (as they were lovingly referred to by then) and I left in the bar. When their conversation turned to the fact that they were going back to a very small, dirty, dingy hotel room with no room service or TV, I graciously offered my very small but clean bachelor apartment. They didn't seem to mind that the only furniture in the room was a queen-sized bed. I had a TV, a few movies, and could bring enough alcohol from the bar to keep us going the rest of the night. They went back to their room, grabbed their bags, and were back at the bar before I finished cleaning.

· · ·   · · ·   · ·

There I was, watching three women getting "comfortable" in my *very* small apartment. Jill, the short brunette, with almond eyes and magnificent hair, was the first out of her clothes, as she started playing bartender wearing just a G-string and a smile. Mandy was next, wearing almost nothing, not caring that her "D" cups couldn't be contained, and Caitlyn, a tall, statuesque brunette, whose only fault was that she considered her breasts too big. *She had an attitude and a mouth that could embarrass anyone within earshot.* We watched movies and drank until we passed out, all four of us, on the queen-sized bed. We woke up at around eight, showered, and off to breakfast at Lani's.

Walking arm in arm, Jill and Mandy on my left, Caitlyn on my right, with what seemed like half the population of Avalon watching from the seawall. We proceeded to Lani's for much needed nourishment, and as we passed, one of the locals called out to ask if I needed any help, just to have Cat spin around and offer, "Thanks... JP is doing a fine job taking care of all of our needs, but thanks for caring." I spent the rest of the week entertaining these lovely women while they were in Catalina, and I spent the next several weekends visiting them in San Francisco.

Truth be known, it was great fun, lots of alcohol, a magnificent experience with three phenomenal women, but *no sex. The San Francisco Three solidified my reputation in Catalina Island for many years to come.*

•   •   •   •   •   •   •   •   •

I was taking a few moments to enjoy Avalon. It is a tiny, picturesque place with a history, and I loved it. The Pavilion, the largest building on the island, is located at the harbor entrance, and is best known for the floating dance floor at its upper level and a small movie theater and museum on the ground floor. It had been *the* destination for the big bands of the '20s and '30s era.

I was sitting on the seawall at the entrance to the harbor, enjoying the orange glow of what was shaping up to be a magnificent sunset, when I was approached by a lovely redhead. I had served her a cocktail the night before, but before I had had a chance to say anything, she had finished her drink and left.

She joined me, silently, just as dusk approached. It was a beautiful, romantic setting—warm, with just the hint of a soft breeze, and the only sound from the ocean was the sound of the waves as they caressed the rocks below me.

She took my hand and led me to a secluded area of the gardens in front of the Pavilion. Ever so softly, she pressed against me and we kissed. Her soft lips had the desired effect, and as her tongue caressed the outline of mine, the kiss grew in intensity. My arousal was becoming quite obvious, and within minutes, she lowered herself between two large bushes in the garden terrace and gently guided me between her legs. For the most part, we were hidden from the view of anyone headed for the museum entrance.

There we were, with me on top and my bare ass bouncing in the warm ocean breeze. The sun was gone and it had just started to get a little darker, when it happened—bam! The spotlights located at the roof level of the Pavilion were on a timer, and it was at that particular moment when they came on, highlighting the garden terraces...*and my bouncing ass.*

It was a very brief, intensely sensuous moment that would have gone relatively unnoticed, except for the fact that, thirty years later, I was visiting the island as a tourist with my wife, son, and seventeen-year-old daughter. As we were walking past that exact spot in front of the Pavilion, I couldn't contain myself and had to share. My daughter, ten years later, still tells her friends about her crazy bartender father having public sex under a spotlight—*and she uses that story every time I try to be "dad" and tell her that she shouldn't be dating bartenders.*

•   •   •   •   •   •   •   •   •

As the winter months were coming to an end, I was getting a little restless and wanted to see the rest of the island. Twin Harbors was on the far end of Catalina Island, isolated, with a population during the off season of only six. The local bar/restaurant/convenience store employed one bartender, two waitresses, and the owner/manager. There was also a boat mechanic and a Los Angeles County deputy sheriff. It is a popular place during the season, with boaters dropping anchor in either of the two harbors to spend a week in seclusion, but during the off season, there was absolutely nothing to do—no boats, no tourists, no action, nothing, but it was the perfect place if you were looking to get away from it all.

I had met Becky at the Marlin Club the night before, a tall, athletic brunette with an attitude (I seemed to be developing a fondness for women with attitude). She suggested that it might be nice to see the rest of the island with me, so I jumped at the chance and made arrangements to rent a jeep for the next day. We left very early the next morning and headed into the interior of the island. Catalina is approximately six miles wide and twenty-four miles long, and as I had mentioned, most of it is set aside as a wildlife preserve. I headed toward Twin Harbors, located at the very end of the island, and the two-hour drive took us through some of the most beautiful parts of Catalina, areas that most of the visitors to the island never had the opportunity to see. A small herd of buffalo slowed our progress, but it gave Becky and I a chance to get better acquainted.

Twin Harbors isn't exactly a bustling community this time of year. By the time we arrived, around ten o'clock in the morning, only the manager of the convenience store and the deputy sheriff were awake. One of the reasons that this area was so popular during the season is that the harbors are isolated, and the only access into them is by boat, or to swim around the rocky cliffs that surround them. Wearing just shorts and T-shirts, we waded along the rocky shoreline, enjoying the view and isolation. I mentioned to Becky that I thought it the perfect opportunity to take a quick dip to cool off, and that it sure was a shame that we hadn't brought our bathing suits. It took Becky almost a second to take the hint, and very quickly, we threw our clothes on to the adjacent rocks.

There we were, enjoying a perfect morning, Becky was on top, having a very good time, and me on the bottom, being used as a damn cushion. We were in the shallow part of the harbor, with the water only a few inches deep. The only sound heard were the waves as they gently caressed the base of the surrounding cliffs, and the very painful groans emanating from me. There was no sandy beach, no soft patch of anything, just big, sharp rocks. The harder we went at it, the more pain I was in, but really, *what man wouldn't sacrifice a little back pain for sex?*

That was then; this is now. My back has never recovered, I never saw Becky again, and over the years, my chiropractor has been paid a small fortune.

• • •   • • •   • • •

Spring on Catalina is much like summer, but without the tourist trade. The weather was getting warmer and there was an air of anticipation as the islanders were getting ready for the start of the season. I was still considered pretty lucky because I had a year-round, full-time job, but could still take time off as requested. Barry and Pat were excellent employers and treated me well. The rest of the "islanders" were pretty much on vacation until the summer season started. The lucky ones still worked on the weekends, but ten of the fourteen restaurants and bars were closed for most of the winter months and wouldn't open until Memorial Day weekend.

I ran "bar tabs" for the out-of-work bartenders and servers during the off season; they were all good for it and would usually have them paid off in less than a month after the season started.

It was a slow, lazy Saturday when a few of us noticed a wedding ceremony being conducted in the parking lot of the Pavilion. Located at the entrance of the harbor, the Pavilion was a popular destination, known for historic parties during the "Big Band" era of the 1920s. We noticed that the local rock band had been engaged to be the entertainment, and it was a beautiful sight. The six band members looked as if they walked right out of the past century, dressed in formal, old style black tuxedos, complete with tails. That is, until the cars they were standing behind drove off, revealing those beautiful tuxedo jackets, covering bathing suits and flip-flops...*only in Catalina.*

Lani was having a little trouble with construction cost overrides and time tables, so it was still questionable as to whether or not I was going to Maui, but I was okay with that, for now. I was having a great time. I had lost most of the weight I had gained as a result of the "arm curls" at the Pubs and I was reaping the benefits, both financially and romantically, of being a bartender on an island resort.

• • •   • • •   • • •

Deanne and her girlfriend arrived on Catalina in March. Although they were born and raised in Long Beach, only a short drive from the San Pedro terminal, it was their first time on the island. After a lazy day on the beach, they found themselves in the Marlin Club in time for last call. I served them a drink and graciously offered to walk them back to their hotel room after I closed up.

During the short walk back to their hotel room, Deanne was more than a little friendly and I was feeling just as frisky, so as her friend entered their room, I pulled Deanne back to me. It was two in the morning, the hotel hallway was quiet, and as her girlfriend closed the door behind her, I looked into Deanne's eyes. There was a hunger in those beautiful eyes, and we had sex against the hotel door. It wasn't pretty, it wasn't romantic, but damn, it was satisfying. Deanne must have felt the same, because the next morning, she called me and came by my apartment. We "hooked up" before breakfast, after breakfast, and the hour before she got on the plane to go home. It was obvious to both of us that we were *extremely sexually compatible.*

I couldn't get her out of my mind, and the following week, I flew to her. She was living with her parents and enjoyed any opportunity to escape. I gave her family a little time to get to know me, but after a few minutes, I made our excuses and told them that we had to leave before we were late for our dinner reservations (we hadn't made any plans, but her parents didn't have to know that). We left their home and drove the two blocks to a small motel that I had passed earlier, and checked in. Once again, it wasn't pretty, it wasn't nice; it was just pure animalistic sex…the type you only read about or see in the movies.

The following week, she came to me. Two days in bed…it was *all* about the sex. The next weekend, I went back to Long Beach and once again picked her up at her parents' house. We drove directly to the same motel, less than four minutes from her house, and after an extremely intense and satisfying session, she sat up and demanded that I take her home. *It was three in the morning, why?* "What's up? Can't we talk about this in the morning?" *Apparently not. She was awfully upset and demanded that I take her home immediately, and I had no idea why.*

She glared at me. "All we do is fuck. We don't go out to dinner, we don't go dancing, we don't go to the movies, we never talk—all we do is fuck."

What could I possibly say? She was right, and my only problem was that I liked it that way. No obligations, no responsibilities, just really great sex.

It was three in the morning. I rolled out of bed, handed her a twenty, and called her a cab. I will be the first one to say that it was not one of my better moments. There was no gallantry involved, and to this day, I am not proud of it. But I was pissed. *It was, after all, very, very, very good sex.*

• • •   • • •   • • •

Frank, local bartender, local bookie, local legend, and he only worked behind the bar because it was easier for his customers to find him. Football, baseball, basketball, it didn't matter. Frank covered all bets, but Frank also had one major problem. Catalina was a playground that many of our local professional athletes enjoyed…normally, without their wives, and over the years, Frank had gotten to know many of them personally. It clouded his judgment, and when it came to game time, he would have trouble picking the winning teams without keeping his emotions out of the equation. Frank's problem also became the island's problem—and the more the athletes "played" on the island, the greater their following. Now, being a New York boy who liked to bet on New York teams, and looking at a game mathematically and not emotionally, Frank, and the islander's problem, helped me pay for more than just one trip to Vegas.

The day after Frank was arrested was one of the busiest days the Marlin Club ever had. The Los Angeles County Sheriff's Department employed a sting operation and set Frank up, along with several of his best clients, which also included my boss, Patricia. The island was in shock as Frank, Pat, and three others were pulled out of their homes, arrested for gambling, and taken back to the mainland to be processed.

By noon the next day, they were all back on the island, and it seemed as if the entire population of Avalon came out of hibernation to get all the details of the big bust. Word got out to the entire island; we had residents come to the bar that day whom we thought were dead—it had been *that* long since anyone had seen them. *It's an island. Any excuse to throw a party seemed to be acceptable.*

●   ●   ●   ●   ●   ●   ●   ●   ●

Memorial Day weekend was only two weeks away and I was ending a pretty rough night shift. From the moment I had started, I was dealing with rude, inconsiderate, drunk customers, and the nasty attitudes were from both tourists and natives alike, Jack in particular. Jack spent his entire life on the island, and for the most part, no one could remember ever having seen him leave. He was also one of the most prejudiced people I had ever met, and he didn't play favorites: he hated everyone. Islanders because they were living off the tourist trade, tourists because they were ruining his island, and the transient labor force (all the bartenders and servers who came to the island to work the season), Jack hated us all.

A bartender's dilemma, do I cut them off? Or keep feeding them drinks to the end of my shift? One of the benefits of being on an island is that you didn't have to worry about anyone driving home drunk, and most of the hotels were within stumbling distance. So for now, I kept the alcohol flowing and did my best to play referee between the islanders who were playing pool and the tourists who were trying to squeeze in. I blinked, just once, and watched as Jack sent a cue ball within inches of a tourist's head. That was it. It wasn't close enough to closing time to give last call, but I had enough. I threw them all out and closed the bar.

I was still trying to get my beauty sleep the next morning when I got a call from Patricia. I had to come down to the bar right away, and not to worry about getting cleaned up. Long before I could see the entrance to the bar, I heard the chants, "Marlin Club, unfair to islanders." Jack and twelve of his friends, with their families, had decided to make a point. They spent the night creating picket signs and were blocking the entrance to the bar. At first, everyone thought it a big joke, but Jack wasn't letting up. This lasted for almost a week, and we all tried reason, common sense, threats, and the law, but nothing worked. Jack was pissed and he was making a point: *he wanted my job.*

Now the last thing I wanted was to put Barry and Pat into a situation— any situation—that would jeopardize what they had spent so much time, energy, and money on. And although I was mad as hell, in *my* eyes, the only remedy seemed for me to leave the island. It was Memorial Day week and the island was filling up with the transient labor force in anticipation of the start of the season. Patricia wouldn't have any trouble finding my replacement, and after several conversations with my friends/employers, Pat and Barry, I left the island on the following day.

I was staying with my friend Jimmy, trying to sort out my life, when I got the call from Pat. The weekend was a disaster and she wanted me back. Barry had pushed his 250 pounds around but it took Patricia telling Jack that she would "shove a two by four up his fat ass if he didn't back off." I agreed to come back for the season and help out, but things were never quite the same.

A Few of Our Regular Customers

I had just started my shift when a customer sat on my bar and ordered an "iced tea…and not that sweet shit." I placed the drink in front of him but couldn't stop staring at him. He looked very familiar, and when I questioned him about it, he just waved me off and told me, "Don't worry about it, Kid. Just keep the drinks coming." After a while, I thought I had recognized him from a '76 gas station commercial, but that wasn't it. He had recently moved to Catalina to get away from the Hollywood scene for a while. After a couple of weeks of serving him his daily dose of "iced teas," we realized that it wasn't the commercials where I knew him from; it was the fact that before he had become an actor/comedian, he spent a few years as a cop in New York City. Not only did he know my uncles, also cops in the city, but my mother's cheesecake was the best he had ever tasted. New York City to Catalina Island, only twenty years and about 3,200 miles away; it sure is a small world.

● ● ●   ● ● ●   ● ● ●

Max Dilman and his crew… Max owned a long-established restaurant called Dilman's on the peninsula, and once a month, he would hire a "small" fishing boat and set sail for Catalina, just Max and twenty of his closest friends. They were on a "mission": to get some sun, to spend a little time on the ocean, to get as drunk as possible, and to still make it back to Dilman's before the change of shift (that way, their wives would never suspect that they had been gone).

• • • • • • • • •

We were about halfway through the season when "Plumber John" became a biweekly regular. He owned a successful plumbing service in Long Beach and he loved the fact that he could get into his new twenty-four-foot speed boat, head it west, and be entering Avalon Harbor in *exactly* thirty-eight minutes. The minute he stepped foot onto his boat, he would call the Marlin Club to give us a heads up that he was on his way, and in *exactly* fifty minutes, he would walk into the bar. If I had his drink sitting on the bar, waiting for him, he stayed all day. If I missed it, even by just a minute, he would have one drink and move on to the next place. John had his wife convinced that he would have to go to the island at least twice a week for service calls because the only plumber on the island was too busy. I can't remember if John even carried his tools with him or not, but he was fun, friendly, and generous, *and needless to say, I never missed a time.*

• • • • • • • • •

"Pipeline John" tried to sail into Avalon Harbor but couldn't; his boat was just too big. The only other time that this had ever happened was when John Wayne tried to sail his yacht into the harbor; he was also stopped. His was even bigger, and, yes, *obviously, there are times that size does matter.*

It was a Saturday and I had switched shifts with Barry so that I could take the night off when Pipeline John walked into the bar with his wife and a "friend." It was early and they were my first and only customers. John and his wife ordered a couple of drinks and I poured a cup of coffee for their friend. When I told them that it would be $3.50, John handed me a $100 bill. I placed his change in front of him, but he just pushed it back to me and told me to keep it. Being the shy person that I am, I graciously said thank you, picked up the $96.50, and continued to set up the bar in anticipation of a busy day, very thankful that I could start my shift so lucratively. I few minutes later, I refreshed the coffee and poured them two more drinks, and once again, John paid with a $100 bill and pushed the change back to me. (Apparently,

John only carried $100 bills and refused to carry anything less. *I was okay with that.*) So far, so good. I had been working almost thirty minutes and I already made $193 in tips; it was going to be a good day.

I learned that John ran a construction crew that was working on the Alaskan pipeline. They would work twelve hours on, twelve hours off for six months at a time, in extremely isolated areas. When they were able to get away, even if it were for just a short time, they would charter a boat and sail the coast. Catalina was their first stop.

John ordered two more drinks, and once again, I was given a $93.50 tip. In one hour, I had received almost $300 in tips and my newfound friends were going to be on the island for a week. I had visions of more trips to Vegas, adding another diamond to one of my rings, and, hell, at his rate, I could ask Barry and Pat if they would like a partner in their bar.

It wasn't until the fourth round when John's "friend" made his presence known. He reached over and picked up the change from the fourth $100 bill and quietly informed me not to be greedy. John's friend was employed by John's wife, to make sure John didn't get too carried away.

• • •　• • •　• • •

The hype, the glory, the excitement…the Annual Marlin Club Golf Tournament was always scheduled on the last weekend of the season. We would have thirty amateur golfers take the shuttle from San Pedro Harbor to Catalina Island for a three-day tournament. They would pile into the Marlin Club as quickly as they could get there from the boat dock, drop off their golf bags in the corner of the bar, and line up for their drinks. That was the closest that any of them came to the actual golf course. Two days later, they would pick up their clubs from the corner of the bar and take the shuttle back to the mainland. (When talking to their wives, I had no doubt that they all had "sub-par" rounds and the golf course was the toughest they had ever played.)

• • •　• • •　• • •

The season had just ended and I was still making a boatload of money, but as I mentioned, things just weren't the same after Jack and friends picketed the bar. I was relieved and pleased when Barry received a phone call from Max Dilman, owner of Dilman's on the peninsula, in Newport Beach. I had gotten to know Max quite well during his infamous trips to the island, and I liked him a lot. His night bartender had been with him for fourteen years, but fell into a diabetic coma over the weekend and died. *Max wanted me for his replacement.*

The mayor came over to ask if I could build him a new school. I traveled miles across our provinces in an effort to find the best lumber. My craftsmen built all of the tables and chairs for our students. Two years I spent to build the finest school in the land, but do they call me Joshua, the school builder? No.

The king came over to ask me to build him the finest castle in the land. Stone from the best quarries, marble from the shores of Italy, ten years in construction. The ramparts would be able to handle a siege from the largest of armies, but do they call me Joshua, the castle builder? No.

The pope came by to ask me to build him a cathedral, and I did. I spent eight years of my life building the most magnificent religious building in our land. Hundreds of stained-glass windows, seating pews for thousands, marble and slate from the best quarries in our land, but do they call me Joshua, the church builder? No.

But you fuck one goat...

Dilman's on the Peninsula

. . .   .

Dilman's is located in Balboa Peninsula, in Newport Beach, California, originally opened by Bill Dilman, and now, thirty years later, was being operated by his son, Max. It has developed a reputation over the years for some of the best, most creative meals in Southern California, with Chef Roger spending the last twenty-two years perfecting his craft. Although the restaurant was known for their prime rib and seafood creations, it was Wild Game Night, the first Tuesday of each month, that put Dilman's on the map. Buffalo, lion, and pheasant were all popular items on the menu.

The success of both the restaurant and bar was also a result of a very seasoned group of bartenders, servers, and kitchen staff. In addition to the chef being there for twenty-two years, the head waitress/bookkeeper had been there twenty-six years, and several of the servers over sixteen years each. In fact, the bartender I had replaced was the new kid on the block; as I had mentioned, he had been there for *only* fourteen years.

As you enter the restaurant, you are greeted by a very large circular bar; it had a center island that housed all of the back bar essentials, including all of the liquor backup, an orange juice machine (the first in the area), and, directly above the center island, a mirror. I had heard stories about how hard it was to work a round bar, and at first glance, it *was* intimidating.

"A round bar is very difficult to work because the bartender can't usually see most of his bar customers. You are always facing away from them, and even when you turn around, the center island is in the way and you can't see the other side of the bar."

One of the reasons why I had accepted the job at Dilman's was that many of their regular clientele (including Max Dilman) were also regular visitors of the Marlin Club on Catalina Island. I had made a major change in employment by coming back to the mainland from the island, but I expected my income to remain consistent. I left Catalina with a little cash and thought it would be a good time to come back to reality (the island, as I finally realized, was too isolated for my taste and I actually missed driving a car). As I left the island, I bought a brand-new corvette and used my VA (Veterans Administration) benefits to buy a house in San Diego, about an hour's drive from the restaurant. I also had to buy a few new clothes to replace the bathing suits and shorts that were the primary uniform of every island resident. I was looking forward to the change in atmosphere and clientele. *I was ready to come back to the real world.*

• • • • • • • •

As usual, I started my first shift a little early, because I wanted to get as familiar with the bar as I could before it started to get busy. I walked behind the bar with a little trepidation, and then I looked up. The mirror was angled in such a way that from the spot where I was standing, the entire bar top was reflected above. I just stood there feeling better about it every minute. If the mirror was used correctly, I would be able to see who needed a drink, or when they were getting close, without having to walk around the center island. The customers sitting at the bar had the wrong angle and had no idea what the mirror's real purpose was, and as I got to know the staff better, I was reasonably certain that they hadn't realized it, either (it was only when actually standing behind the bar that you could *see* the bar top).

I started to experiment with the different angles from the different locations behind the bar, and, as it turned out, it was pretty sweet. With a little practice, I could be standing in my "well," look up as customers entered the lounge from the doors in front of me, and then glance at the mirrors above to determine when the customers were ready to order their drinks. An added bonus for both me and the "regular customer" was that I would actually make their drink, and with some very good timing, place it in front of the customer at the exact moment he would put his ass on the stool. I perfected this as I got to know the regulars better, because I would know what they wanted, how many they were going to have, and when I should bring their checks without ever asking them.

By the end of my first day, I felt pretty good about myself and I asked if it were okay to order some dinner. To my surprise, I was allowed to order anything on the menu, anything, so I ordered the prime rib. My new employer, Max, joined me at the bar after my shift was over to ask me how I liked my first day. I was just about to sample my dinner when I looked over at him and mentioned that most restaurants I had worked in would only allow the staff to eat the daily specials or some of the inexpensive menu items, but never the high-end portion of the menu.

Max looked at me and pointed to the cash register behind the bar. "You see that register? That's my money in that register, and you have control of my money...you can have anything on the menu that you want."

For the first twelve months that I was there, six nights a week, I ordered prime rib, but even I could get too much of a good thing. So one day, before the kitchen closed, I ordered a hamburger, a plain, greasy, no frills hamburger. *Damn, it tasted good.*

In addition to taking care of *his* money, Max only had two rules that I had to worry about. There were only two reasons for not showing up for a shift: first, if I were too drunk to stand, and second, if I were getting laid, end of story. No other excuse was acceptable. This was going to be a very interesting opportunity.

•   •   •   •   •   •   •   •   •

Wild Game Night is scheduled for the first Tuesday of every month, and had been a successful event at Dilman's for many years. Our chef was phenomenal, and he would get as creative with the menu as possible, while staying within the guidelines of the law. That isn't so easy when you're offering items on a menu that, for the most part, are on the endangered species list, but he always managed to find a purveyor who offered buffalo and lion. Every once in a while, he would throw in pheasant, boar, or snake; it was a very interesting dining experience and we were packed for every event.

It was my fourth Wild Game Night and we were all pumped up and ready to go. It was also the only night of the month when we needed two bartenders. George was a frail sixty-year-old man, but he had spent enough years behind the bar that I found him to be extremely competent and useful. What he lacked in speed, he more than made up for with his knowledge and experience; he knew instinctively what had to be done, what I needed for backup, and he easily managed the bar behind me, so that I could stay focused on all of the servers' drink orders, and the bar section directly in front of me. As I was finishing my prep work, I looked around. *It was getting very busy.*

I had just walked behind the bar when I saw George collapse in front of his station, and about five minutes later, the paramedics were wheeling George to the ambulance (thank God the fire station was just a few minutes away). I looked around and felt like throwing up; the busiest night of the month was about to start in about an hour, and I was one bartender short. I immediately converted my workstation into a service bar and asked Max to remove the bar stools in front of me. I then set up my well with as many extra glasses and ice buckets as I could find. Once it started, I was going to have my head in the ice for about four solid hours and I couldn't leave anything to chance. Max took up a position next to my impromptu service bar and started to power down his vodka rocks. He would sit for hours, watching his customers and keeping an eye on his bartenders, but I knew that it was the number of times that we would put money into his cash register that really turned him on.

We were getting busier. It was already two deep in the bar and my servers were ordering drinks two trays at a time. I was in "the zone," moving quickly, smoothly, and keeping up with the demand. The busier I got, the better the service seemed to be; servers and customers alike were having a good time watching me work the bar. Later, I was told that "it **was** a thing of beauty," but I was way too busy to notice…or care.

I was in the process of making four margaritas. I had a bottle of tequila and a bottle of triple sec, two bottles in each hand, when it happened. One of the bottles in my left hand slipped and it hit a couple of the glasses that I had set up. My hand came down on one of the pieces and it sliced open my hand while the rest of the shattered glass fell into the ice bin. I immediately started to use one of my backup ice buckets and was pouring drinks with one hand as the blood was pouring out of the other. As the drink orders were starting to pile up, I looked over at a very bleary-eyed Max and almost died when he reminded me of his two basic rules: "Are you drunk? Are you getting a blow job back there? No? Then I expect you to do your job."

I was fighting a losing battle trying to keep up with the drink orders when I took a step back and asked one of my waitresses to wrap my hand to stop the bleeding. While this was going on, one of my regular customers jumped behind the bar and started to clean out the ice bin to get ready for some clean ice. They both finished at about the same time and I was back in business, granted, with only one hand, but I was still able to pour.

It turned out to be a very good night. Everyone must have felt sympathy for the poor, one-handed bartender, because both servers and customers over-tipped. *I casually thought that I might want to try that one-handed stuff more often.*

A Few of Our Regular Customers

I had a retired US Air Force general who loved to talk about the twenty years that he spent in the military. He would talk and expound on his adventures for as long as someone was willing to buy him a drink. For someone so successful, I thought our general had the "shortest arms" I had ever seen. Everyone loved him, and he milked that for all it was worth. Who wouldn't buy a member of our armed forces a drink, let alone a general? But his "short arms" never seemed long enough to reach the money in his pockets. In the eighteen months that I worked at Dilman's, I could not remember a time, not one, when he actually paid for a drink.

Years later, when he passed away, many of our regular customers, including Dilman's staff, showed up for the ceremony. Because of his military rank, we all sat there, expecting to see an honor guard, complete with a twenty-one gun salute. But when the pastor finished his eulogy, he gave recognition of our friend, and the *four years* he had spent in the service as a US Air Force *sergeant*. The general had pulled off one hell of a con, for most of his life, and to celebrate it, Max threw one hell of a party.

· · ·   · · ·   · · ·

Max Dilman's "crew" was the gentlemen who started every day at six in the morning with Max, a core group of Max's friends who really loved the juicer that he had installed on the back bar. Apparently, the fresh orange and grapefruit juice was something they all looked forward to (that, and the vodka that came with it).

All of Max's morning regulars were considered retired, and very wealthy. The morning meetings with Max seemed to be the highlight of their day. To give you an idea of what I'm talking about, one of these gentlemen owned three car dealerships, another owned two yacht dealerships, and one was in real estate, who seemed to have inherited a quarter mile of Wilshire Boulevard in Los Angeles at a very young age and had never held a *real* job, *ever*, and he had just celebrated his seventy-ninth birthday. Max's "crew" was a pretty impressive group.

· · ·   · · ·   · · ·

Diane worked at a local Mexican restaurant, also in the "peninsula." She was a "professional" cocktail server, attractive, single, and trouble. It was not unusual for her to decide that the end of a busy shift was more than enough reason to throw a celebration. At any given time, she could swing by Dilman's after closing her bar and ask for a drink, sex, or company on a quick road trip at two in the morning; Las Vegas for breakfast, or San Francisco for brunch, you just never knew.

My favorite "celebration" occurred once every two or three weeks; her bar would close at around midnight, just like everyone else's on the peninsula, and she would head over to Dilman's for last call (I always tried to keep it open at least until one-thirty every night). She would wait for the last customer to leave before making sure that the curtains on all of the windows in the lounge were wide open. Dilman's was located on the corner of the block, and the windows in the lounge faced two busy streets, and Diane was taking being an exhibitionist to a whole new level. She loved having sex on top of the bar, while looking up at the ceiling mirror, knowing that every car that passed by would have the *opportunity* to see us. I was reasonably sure that we were never "caught," but traffic did seem to noticeably slow down on the nights we were "celebrating."

• • • • • • • • •

We'll call him "Dan," someone who made it into the restaurant exactly once every two weeks. For the entire time I worked there, he was definitely considered a regular. It wasn't until much later when I found out that Dan was referred to as a "spotter," someone employed to come to a bar and act as a customer, in an effort to "spot" anything the boss considered bad, from stealing money to bad service. His job was to catch us in the act and write us up for management review.

It was obvious that Dan didn't like me at all, but he could never catch me doing anything wrong. His only beef was when he would sit at my bar for hours (along with every other regular customer), but never once saw me write down a drink order or close out a tab, and until he did, he wouldn't be able to accuse me of giving away a drink or stealing. His job was to watch what I was ringing up on the register, but he would normally have to leave before I did and the only tab I would have closed would have been his. My Hof's Hut training really paid off in spades for this one. I had been able to remember 100 drinks at a time; Dilman's bar only had twenty-two bar stools…piece of cake.

Of note, my boss, Max Dilman, was the recipient of the worst bar write-up of the restaurant's history; he always gave away drinks when he was behind the bar, and had been known to take money out of the register for no apparent reason. It's a good thing the "spotter" was on Max's payroll and not the other way around.

• • • • • • • • •

My favorite was Richard, who spent most of his life growing up in the peninsula; he has been a "regular" at Dilman's since he was five years old. Richard, a welder by trade, was often unemployed for short periods, and during those times, Max always made sure that he would have something to eat and drink. He would sit at his favorite table, dine with us, drink with us, and then pay his tab, *with a bad check*. And once a month, Richard's dad would come in to cover any shortages and thank Max for taking care of his son.

Richard had an idea, a concept, and he thought that by using his welding skills, he could create "modular" office furniture. He convinced three of his friends to invest $5,000 each to help him through the development stage, and about a year later, he filed patents on what he had created, and the rest is history. I met Richard during the time of his life when he was reaping the benefits of his creation and he no longer needed to work.

I was fortunate in that Dilman's was the only lounge in the peninsula that would stay open until two in the morning, every day. The rest of the bars and restaurants in the area would normally close at around midnight, which gave me an excellent late-night rush.

It was one-thirty in the morning and my bar was filled with the local bartenders and servers who had already ended their shifts. Richard came in just as I was about to give last call, and as he looked around, he ordered a round of drinks for the entire bar. Just as I finished setting everyone up with their drinks, Richard asked if I wouldn't mind doing it again. I looked at the bartenders and servers sitting in my bar and decided that they would have no problem finishing their drinks before the two o'clock deadline. Another five minutes passed and Richard did it again. "Richard, there's no way anyone is going to finish that many drinks before two o'clock." But he insisted that I pour them anyway. I set everyone up for a third time and started to get the bar ready to close. As good as my customers were, they couldn't finish them all, and when they started to close out their tabs and leave, they just pushed the drinks left in front of them toward me. By two o'clock, everyone was gone except for Richard, and I asked him why he did it. (He had purchased three rounds of drinks for twenty-four customers in less than ten minutes, knowing that they wouldn't be able to finish them. I was curious.) He just looked at me, smiled, and said, "I enjoy a good show and wanted to watch you wash the glasses."

When I finished the glasses, he threw me an extra $100 for my trouble and left the bar. He really did "invent" modular office furniture, and he was obviously running out of ideas to help him spend his money, *but who was I to complain?*

A Few of My Friends

Kelly T. owned and operated a very successful hair salon in Balboa Peninsula, and had been a regular at Dilman's for almost twenty years. He was also my hairstylist, and once a month, I would visit Kelly at his salon, and once a week, he would visit me at Dilman's. Not a bad trade off. Denise was a very voluptuous, vivacious woman, almost five-foot nothing, with blond hair; she was also Kelly's girlfriend and worked as a manicurist at the salon. On one of my trips to see Kelly, he was running a little late with his last appointment, and

Denise offered to keep me busy and do my nails while I waited. About a minute later, I was hooked. Having this little slice of heaven working on my hands as I was staring at her ample cleavage became the highlight of my day. It was truly a magnificent view, and she knew it. From that day on, I always booked a manicure directly *after* my haircut.

On one of my visits to see Kelly, he told me that he and Denise would be going to St. Thomas, in the Virgin Islands, for a much needed vacation, and that I shouldn't be too surprised if they came back as husband and wife. The day they came back, Kelly called me to let me know that they had, in fact, been married while they were gone, but the big news was that they were moving to the island, effective immediately. On the day they returned, Kelly sold his salon to one of his hairstylists and rented his house to another; he wasn't wasting any time.

While they were on vacation, Kelly had rented a yacht, complete with a pastor, so that he could surprise Denise with an ocean wedding. The captain anchored his vessel just off a small, isolated beach to perform the ceremony. The setting was perfect, and as the happy couple stood in front of the pastor, Kelly could see out of the corner of his eye that all of the sunbathers on the beach had stopped what they were doing to watch the ceremony. As the pastor announced, "I now pronounce you husband and wife. You may kiss the bride," the beach exploded with cheers.

As Kelly and his new bride looked over at them, they realized that it was a "topless beach," and all Kelly could focus on was the number of bare breasts bouncing in front of him. Kelly had found his nirvana, and on the trip back to the harbor, the pastor told him that he was making $50,000 a year performing weddings, and another $50,000 a year playing with a local jazz band on the weekends. Kelly was hooked. By the time he and Denise left the island, he had secured a hairstylist job at the local hair salon and Denise was going to be their new manicurist.

The end result: we were packing up his furniture to put into storage, and I was forced to start looking for a new hairstylist. *I will sure miss those manicures.*

• • • • • • • •

Debbie stopped by one evening to say hi. She had visited me at the Marlin Club several times and we tried to hook up any chance we could, but this was the first time she ever made it to Dilman's. She was tiny, with extremely short black hair and a very shy personality. She was, as the saying goes, "cute as a button."

I had first met her years earlier, while she was working as a hostess at a nightclub called Gatsby's Rendezvous. A friend of mine brought me to the club and introduced me as *Giuseppe Antonio Pietro Roberto Palmese*. She showed us to our table, but by the time we finished dinner, she was gone.

A few nights later, I stopped by, and as soon as I walked through the door, she said, "Good evening, Giuseppe Antonio Pietro Roberto Palmese. Are you here for dinner or just cocktails?"

Now that *was* impressive. No one had ever taken the time to remember my whole name before. The following day, I sent her a dozen roses. The next day, I sent two dozen roses. On the third day, she received a bird of paradise. On the fourth day, a dozen orchids. On the fifth day, her manager called me to say *enough*; she was having trouble functioning with all the flowers around her hostess station. And besides, Debbie had been "**mine**" after the first two deliveries.

I went to Gatsby's to see her on the following day, and we spent that night, and the following weekend, together. As I was leaving for Catalina Island on the following week, it was a very short, but intense, romance. She did manage to see me while I was on the island, but it was too inconvenient of a trip for her to visit more than a couple of times a year. I hadn't seen her for almost a year when she walked into Dilman's. It was like time had stopped and I hadn't realized how much I had missed her. She waited for me to get off shift and we spent the night together. It was her way of saying good-bye. *She was pregnant...engaged to be married...and she needed to borrow $300.*

Six years later, I was managing a mortgage company when I received a call from an appraisal company soliciting my business. I picked up the phone and answered, "This is Giuseppe Antonio Pietro Roberto Palmese. How may I help you?"

There was a long pause on the other end of the phone, and then I heard a shy, quiet voice ask, "Is that you, Joe?"

Debbie and I had lunch the next day to catch up...and, yes, she was still "cute as a button." Her little girl was obviously the highlight of her life, and she was now single. But after all that time, *all I could think about was the $300 she still owed me.*

* * *   * * *   * * *

Many, many years later, I stopped by Dilman's with a friend of mine to have a drink and see how the place was doing. Nothing had changed, from the décor of the bar to Max Dilman sitting in front of his bartender, watching his register. I bought Max a drink—vodka rocks, of course—and went over to say hi. He looked up at me, grinned, and said, "Damn, you were the fastest bartender who ever worked for me. You still in the business, George?" So much for lasting impressions and my ego.

So this couple decided to take their eight-year-old son, Joey, to the zoo. As they came upon the elephant exhibit, Joey pointed to the elephant and asked, "Mom, what's that big thing hanging from the elephant?"

"Why, that's the elephant's trunk, Son," his mother replied.

Joey then asked, "Mom, what's that other big thing hanging from the elephant?"

"Why, Son, that's the elephant's tail."

Joey listened intently but was still curious. "Mom, what's that **other** big thing hanging there?"

Slightly embarrassed, his mom softly said, "Oh, that's nothing, Son."

Joey, more than a little frustrated, turned to his dad. "Dad, what's that big thing hanging from the elephant?"

His dad looked over and said, "Joey, that's the elephant's trunk."

"Dad, I know where the trunk is, and the tail, but I want to know what that **other** big thing is…hanging there between the trunk and the tail."

"Why, Son, that's the elephant's penis."

After careful consideration, Joey said, "Dad, why did Mom tell me that it was nothing?"

"Well, Son," his dad stated as he proudly hitched up his trousers, "your mother's been spoiled."

Gatsby's Rendezvous

• • • • • • • • •

Gatsby's Rendezvous was an impressive restaurant and nightclub by anyone's standards. It was patterned after the novel *The Great Gatsby* by F. Scott Fitzgerald, and as you entered the lobby area, you realize just how big 25,000 square feet really is. A thirty-stool bar was off to the right with an area set aside for four custom backgammon tables. To the left, there were several cocktail sections that were on different levels, overlooking the stage and dance floor. It was a large stage that included a disc jockey booth large enough for two.

The restaurant area alone, situated at the back of the room, had a seating capacity of 160, and included a separate service bar section, set up for two bartenders. The main bar was designed with three waitress and four bartending stations, and it only took a few minutes behind the bar to realize that whoever designed it had spent some time as a bartender. The refrigeration doors on the back bar was facing the right direction, the back bar itself had ample room for liquor backup and glassware, and the "wells" in each bartending station had large ice bins with speed racks on each end and in the front (a good bartender could pump out some serious alcohol). From the dining room and the bar, to the kitchen and restrooms, everything about the place was large and impressive, just like the book.

• • • • • • • • •

It was my first day, and here I was, the new bar manager of one of the most popular nightclubs in the county, and we were about to run out of liquor. I was taking over an operation where the partners were ripping each other off, there were bill collectors lining up at my office door, and the three largest restaurant and bar suppliers had cut off our credit. Without credit, we would have to pay for everything on a cash-and-carry basis, and I was told there was no cash.

My new employer, Al, an attorney by trade, had found out that his partner wasn't taking care of the business; he was probably stealing, and supplies were missing. There were rumors that his partner had serious connections in some dishonest endeavors, and as an attorney, Al was very concerned…and he was out of money. He had just spent the last three months legally dissolving his partnership when I was asked to help. Two of the bartenders quit when the now ex-partner was physically removed the day before, and the rest of the bartenders and cocktail servers hadn't been paid in several weeks. *Great first day—and it wasn't noon yet.*

The books indicated that a liquor shipment, a little over $10,000, had been delivered on December 27 in anticipation of the New Year's Eve party that had been scheduled. I knew the party had been a success, but this was only January 2, and for all intents and purposes, the liquor room was empty (unless you count the two bottles of Crème De Cocoa and one bottle of green Crème De Menthe). The liquor in the bartender's wells was okay to open the place, but the back bar was half empty, and this was a very busy club. The current liquor on hand wouldn't last two days.

To make matters worse, I had just finished taking the inventory when I walked into the main bar, into a room of giants. No less than twenty very large bodybuilder types were having a really good time harassing the few patrons in the room. Everywhere I looked, there was a 300-pound giant of a man pushing someone around. I tried diplomacy and got pushed around; I tried threats and they just laughed. It was obvious that they were either so well connected that they could do whatever they wanted to anyone they chose or they just didn't give a damn about the consequences. It was as if the cast of *The Sopranos* had stopped by for drinks, and they were all invited guests of the now ex-partner of my current employer, the same ex-partner who probably moved the contents of our liquor room to his garage over the long weekend.

I was more than just a little afraid. It was my first day on the job, and although I spent the last several years building a pretty solid resume as a professional bartender, my management skills were still in their infancy. I knew, deep down in my heart, that I was about to get my ass kicked. So I did what every kid would do when he gets in a little over his head: I went back to my office and called my mom.

I was nervous and immediately went off on my mom, hoping to get the fear out of my system before I had to go back out into the bar and face the "300-pound club." With a little luck, my mother would calm me down before I lost control of the situation and wind up with a few beefy bodies using me for a trampoline. I briefly mentioned to her that it was a good thing that I didn't carry a gun, because I probably would use it right about now (just to scare them, of course). My mother paused for a moment, and then said, "No, Son, that's what we have family for."

All I could mutter pitifully was, "We do?"

Apparently, my dear, sweet little Italian mother is the one responsible for keeping the family records, including the uncles whom none of the younger children were allowed to talk about or to. She told me to sit tight while she made a few calls. About ninety minutes had gone by when one of my "uncles" called me at the club, asked a few questions, and said he would get back to me in the morning. I went back out into the bar and focused on coming up with an idea to supply the bar with alcohol while trying to keep everybody safe.

The next day, my uncle called me at my apartment. The boys in my bar weren't connected, but my uncle could have two hundred "soldiers" there by the end of the day to take care of my problem. But I had better make sure that I *really* needed them. I told him that I would get back with him and called my mom. She told me to make sure, very sure, that I needed the family's help. There was no talk of threats or obligations, or who any of these people actually were. It was just my mom telling me that she hadn't raised a flipping coward, and that maybe, I had moved out of the house too soon. I had better be *really* sure that I needed the help. So thanks to my mom, I got my balls on and told my uncle that I would be able to handle it, but I thanked him for the concern and went to work. Hopefully, he would be pleased that my mom would bake for him one of her famous cheesecakes to say thank you for his time.

●　●　●　　　●　●　●　　　●　●　●

The following morning, as I was about to open the front door of the nightclub, I was greeted by an older gentleman who introduced himself as an officer of the court. He was a retired Orange County sheriff who had been employed to collect the past due debts owed to some of our creditors. Fondly referred to as a "keeper," because it was his job to "keep" our money, he would insure that our opening bank was $200, then sit in front of the cash register for the entire day, and at the change of shift, take the entire proceeds of the day, leaving us with our opening $200.

After I introduced him to the staff at an impromptu meeting, I had a few private employee meetings of my own. Our first order of business was to figure out how we could generate cash flow and *keep it* from the *keeper* (I wouldn't be able to pay for supplies "cash and carry" without cash). The second order of business was to handle the bodybuilders, who I knew would start coming to the club at any moment. The least of my worries was the actual operation of the club. It had only been a couple of days, but it was obvious to me that I had a pretty competent crew. My bartenders were experienced, friendly, and seemed to have a reasonable following, and my cocktail servers were good-looking, seasoned professionals with attitude.

They had all been working this club for years and I thought it best to let them continue with going about their business as usual. As our new best friend, the "keeper," settled in at the bar to start his shift, our bodybuilder friends came back. I had to deal with them, and now that I had rested and was using a little common sense, I asked them a few pertinent questions. I offered them a round of drinks and sat down right in the middle of them. "First, how many of you have worked at Gatsby's Rendezvous before, as either a server or bouncer?" Most had. "Second, is the ex-partner paying you to come in and mess with the business?" No, and, in fact, he still owed some of them wages. And finally, "Most of you seem to know, and like, everyone working here, so why would you want to screw with their livelihood?" They didn't.

The remedy was actually pretty simple. Those who needed the extra income, I rehired as bouncers; those who couldn't afford a drink, I offered them a house tab that they could cover after they worked a couple of shifts for me. That allowed them all to relax and spend more time with the staff. After all, that *was* why they were there. As they were all getting reacquainted and starting to have a good time, my head waitress, Jean, pulled me aside to discuss our other problem.

• • •   • • •   • • •

Jean was definitely the waitress in charge, a tall brunette with shortly cropped, unruly hair and an attitude that I truly enjoyed. She had what I would describe as a lithe, athletic body, with long, beautiful legs. She liked the way I handled the 300-pound club and had made the decision that our current situation called for her, as head waitress, to be a little more aggressive in helping me to get Gatsby's back on track. She had been there for almost three years and had not been a fan of the last management group.

As I listened intently, she explained that in her past life, she had been a hooker (not a prostitute who waited for the calls from a manager or a book of business she had built up), but a hooker, who worked the streets and did whatever it took to survive. I will admit that for a brief moment, I was tempted to ask her to do whatever it took to help with our "keeper," but then, common sense (and my morality?) kicked in. And as I watched our little old man at the bar, I had a better idea.

Jean's uniform was a low-cut, tightly fitting buttoned affair that, when a button was left undone, the result was a very good view of her perky breasts... and she *always* had the top one undone. I mentioned to her that our keeper seemed to be mesmerized every time she went up to the bar, and if we could keep him from watching the register, we might actually be able to stash some cash. Without so much as a nod that she understood, she unbuttoned the top two buttons and stood next to the keeper. From the way she was leaning, our man had the perfect view of an extremely prominent nipple, inches away from his face. When he caught himself staring, he looked up at Jean's face, totally embarrassed, but she just smiled. Our keeper was in heaven, and I know that even if his life depended on it, he wasn't going to take his eyes off that erect nipple.

Jean was definitely a pro, and if she needed to leave for any reason at all, she would motion to have one of her other servers take her place. The entire afternoon, I watched as my bartenders gave new meaning to the term "stealing," ringing up only one drink out of five and putting the rest of the cash in their tip jars. At the end of their shift, they came into the office and just handed me the jars.

This went on for almost two weeks, and from the attitude of our keeper, you would have thought that this had been the greatest sexual experience of his life. Thanks to Jean, her girls, and the experience level of my bartenders, the keeper collected enough to pay the creditors who had hired him, but on our terms, not his, and we were able to pay for the liquor and supplies we needed to stay in business.

• • •　• • •　• • •

My bookkeeper, RC, was also responsible for our marketing, and she gave a lot of thought into throwing a grand opening party to celebrate the new management of Gatsby's, and St. Patrick's Day was just around the corner. To help promote the event, we decided to take our employees, all twenty-two of them, on a Sunday afternoon "pub crawl" across the Balboa Peninsula. The entire length of the peninsula was lined with no less than thirty bars and restaurants, from little hole-in-the-wall dumps to four-star dining rooms, and we were planning on visiting *all* of them. The uniform of the day would be green Gatsby's T-shirts, white shorts, and roller skates (we thought that the skates would make sure that we could hit all the clubs faster). Lynn was one of my managers and lived on Balboa Island. We would all meet at her house at around ten.

On the chosen day, we all gathered at Lynn's house for a quick Sunday brunch before strapping on our skates; a little food, copious amounts of champagne, and we were ready. Dilman's on the peninsula was our first stop; Max, always the perfect host, allowed us to roll right into the bar and set us up with Mimosa's (the fresh juice machine was worth every penny). Next was the Pavilion, across the street, for Bloody Marys, then margaritas at the Mexican restaurant next store, then on to the restaurant on the pier, where they offered us shots of tequila. It was a great start: four restaurants in thirty minutes (the roller skates sure made it easy).

For the rest of the afternoon, we rolled (or skidded) into every place in the Balboa Peninsula with a liquor license; only one wouldn't let us in with our skates on, but the rest of them had no problem letting us make complete fools of ourselves. We started with twenty-two of my employees and finished up with twenty; two were missing in action, but by the end of the day, it didn't matter. All of us were exhausted, and more than a little drunk, but we had a blast. The next weekend was our grand opening party, and it was a huge success, with more than half of the customers coming in as a result of our "Peninsula Pub Crawl" event on St. Patty's Day.

● ● ●   ● ● ●   ● ● ●

Keith proved to be one of my better bartenders, always pleasant and personable, and very competent. Debbie was one of my senior servers, and my "go-to" gal; whether I needed coverage in the dining room or the nightclub, she was always there to help. They were two of my best, and they were a couple. They had been living together for about a year when Keith decided to make it permanent, and when he asked her if she would marry him, she quickly accepted. They wanted the ceremony to be at Gatsby's. It was where they first met and fell in love, and they wanted it to happen *now*.

RC came through again, and on the following week, Keith and Debbie became mister and missis. The ceremony was very nice and RC arranged one hell of a party. A couple of weeks later, Keith and Debbie flew back to Las Vegas to make their announcement to his family, and when they came back, they gave me their two-week notice. Keith's father was editor of a Las Vegas newspaper, and when he learned of his son's marriage, he decided that his son and new wife should have a new start, so for a wedding present, he gave them a tanning salon, located in downtown Las Vegas.

● ● ●   ● ● ●   ●

It was March, and the news on the street was all about a club in Los Angeles County that started to promote an all-male review, apparently the first in the country (but I never did confirm that). Every Wednesday night, for a small cover charge, women would line up in front of Chippendales for the opportunity to watch good-looking men dance and take off their clothes. It wasn't considered socially or morally acceptable, and all the "press" about it seemed to be bad. But it didn't seem to stop the women.

The first thirty minutes of our next staff meeting was all about Chippendales, and by the end of the meeting, I was almost convinced that our next move to promote Gatsby's was to offer a show along the same lines. RC was responsible for setting up any special events, and she wanted a shot at it.

Now, RC is an impressive woman, a larger version of that Halloween icon, "Elvira—Mistress of the Dark," and because she *was* so impressive, and more than just a little intimidating, she usually got her way. She thought that we could do it better, and by the end of the week, she had me convinced. We would offer the *same* all-male review using the now infamous Chippendales dancers; they would perform on Wednesday nights at Chippendales and Saturday and Sunday afternoons at Gatsby's. She also had a few friends working in a new show in Las Vegas, called "Boylesque," and it didn't take much of an effort to schedule them as our opening act.

We had the club, 25,000 square feet of it. We already had the license that allowed us to offer live entertainment, and the dancers and opening act were ready. RC set it up with two shows each day, the first at four o'clock in the afternoon and the second at six. We set up May 1 as our premier, and all that was left for me to do was to hire a few more servers and an extra bartender.

This all-male review was new, and it seemed like we were going to be only the second club to offer it. One of my many concerns during all this was the staff necessary to make it all work. Up to this point, a server's qualifications did not include working topless, and according to the ladies we interviewed, this was an area that needed quite a bit of attention. We *had to have* male servers, not female, and male cocktail servers weren't a common item.

The required uniform was going to be black pants, no shirt, white cuffs, a white collar, and black bow tie (a simple white shirt and a pair of scissors was all it took for the cuffs and collar). My bouncer/bodybuilder group was the first to offer their services, but not one of them had any real experience in the business. That would have been a disaster just waiting to happen. As the opening was drawing near, I started having nightmares about a group of bodybuilders flexing their muscles while 200 women were *trying* to buy drinks.

RC and I combined our talents for the interview process: she picked them for their looks and I would check their cocktail skills. As we got closer to our premier on May 1, I was still short one server and had to go back to the original group of bodybuilders. Tony worked for me as a bouncer on the weekends and worked for a restaurant supply company during the week (at least he worked in the industry), so I gave him the chance. I had a few more interviews set up for bartenders, my serving staff was ready, and I was almost finished converting a full-service kitchen into a dressing room for six female impersonators.

I was running out of time. The Friday before our opening, I was still one bartender short and had only one interview left. His name was Kurt, and when he handed me his resume, all I could do was stare. He was selling me hard on how good he was and his resume *was* impressive, but I just couldn't stop staring...*at the man who took a lot of pride in teaching me how to steal five years earlier*. I just sat there and let him finish selling himself. When done, I looked at him and asked, "Kurt, you don't remember me, do you?" He looked at me a little harder, but I had changed. My hair was longer and straighter, and I had a full mustache, a much different look than the short, curly haired, clean shaven ex-marine who he had worked with.

When he still had no clue, I offered, "Hof's Hut, five years ago." He just picked up his resume and left...no good-byes, no thank you for the opportunity, nothing. *How rude.* It looked as if I was out of options. I was going to be the final bartender, and *thank God* we had an enclosed service bar section that was not in plain view of the bar patrons. I knew what I looked like without a shirt on and I wasn't prepared to be critiqued by the intimidating RC.

RC was good. The "boys" from Las Vegas drove out for breakfast that Saturday morning and they would spend most of the day setting up their "dressing room" and makeup stations, and the dancers would be arriving at around one o'clock to get ready. The doors were scheduled to open at two, to allow everyone time to get settled and get the drink orders in before the show started. We had over 200 women lined up outside, ready to enter at $4 a head, and I was hoping that the staff was ready.

I unlocked the doors and the "ladies" rushed in, throwing their money at my cashier as they passed in a stampede to get as close to the stage as possible. As the room filled up, I began to realize just how much my "waiters" didn't know. Tony was our first casualty; his section was a small balcony section overlooking the stage with only four tables in it (I had thought that he wouldn't have any trouble with such a small group). He walked over to take the ladies' orders, flexing and posing as he went; as a bodybuilder, he was in his element, and it was obvious that he was having a very good time. He wrote down the drink orders for all four tables and presented them to the bartender...*he was really proud of himself*.

The bartender made the drinks and Tony arranged them on two trays. He picked them up, one in each hand, lifted them high over his head, and "strutted" back to the balcony. He was definitely in his glory. There he stood, in the middle of his cocktail section, bodybuilder physique, arms raised high, holding both trays of drinks above his head, every muscle in his body on display, with his chiseled "six pack" teasing the women at the tables. Then it happened: our guests were impatient and got tired of waiting for the dancers to start, so they took it upon themselves to start without them. Poor Tony, with both hands filled with two trays of drinks, trying hard not to spill them, and the ladies at his surrounding tables had his pants around his ankles in less time than it took him to realize what had happened. There he stood, basically naked except for the white cuffs and collar, holding two trays of drinks. *It was not one of his better moments, but that being said, he didn't spill a drop.*

When the dust settled, we all realized that we survived the first weekend, but just barely. I needed to spend a little more time working on the kitchen/dressing room/makeup counters for "Boylesque," and with the exception of Tony's opening act, it went pretty smoothly. We weren't quite busy enough for me to work the service bar, so I was able to keep my shirt on, and I spent most of my time on the floor, backing up the servers. Everyone made a lot of money on that first weekend, and the entire staff was already planning on how to do it better next week.

The word was out, and by Wednesday of the following week, we had over three hundred reservations for the next weekend. Once again, the doors were unlocked and our guests rushed in, trying to get close to the stage. But this time, we were better prepared and the reservations were a huge help.

RC had reserved the dance floor in front of the stage for a few "invited guests," a group of dancers from several of the topless bars in the area. (I will always have a soft spot in my heart for these professional women.) The room filled up and we were standing room only in a very short period of time. As the show started, the ladies were pumped up, especially our invited guests on the dance floor. Maybe because this venue was new, maybe because it was the girls getting even, but when the third dancer hit the stage, the "professionals" in front could no longer contain themselves.

It became a race to the stage to see who was going to make a souvenir of the dancer's G-string—and then it was a race to see which officer of the law could get their badges out faster. There were no less than four undercover vice cops in the audience, and that little exhibition just earned me my first indecent exposure ticket, courtesy of the local police force. The dancer was pissed because his ability to earn tips just ended, and I was in shock, because, as the manager of the club, I was held accountable, which was why both the dancer **and** I received the indecent exposure tickets. The good news? *They didn't stop the show.*

On Monday morning, RC handed me a copy of the local newspaper, and there we were: the complete centerfold of the paper was covered with pictures of our club, our patrons, and the dancers. RC was proudest of the small picture in the left-hand corner. There she was, RC's little sixty-five-year-old mom, knitting what looked like a small blanket, but taking the time to gently tuck a dollar bill in the G-string of one of the dancers. *You couldn't buy advertising like that.*

It was a good thing that we were offering two shows each on both Saturday and Sunday, because by Thursday, we had over 400 reservations. We decided to take advantage of the situation and expand the show. The Chippendales crew added a few more dancers and I extended the hours to two three-hour shows; our doors would open at noon.

It was also payday, so I asked my crew to come in a little early to pick up their checks before they got ready for the shows. There I was, trying to hand out their checks, but they wouldn't take them; they just snickered at me, and finally, they told me why. I guess I had been too busy bouncing between the service bar, keeping an eye on the ever-present vice cops, and solving problems that I hadn't noticed that my crew had developed what they were calling as "fuck tickets."

In addition to making very good tips for the weekend, they offered our guests a simple napkin, with their name, phone number, and $20 written on the front; our guests couldn't buy them fast enough. My loyal staff was getting laid as much as two to three times a day, every day, and between their tips and the "fuck tickets," they had made so much money that they felt guilty accepting my meager wages.

Ladies gone wild doesn't come close to describing the behavior of the women coming to our club, and it was only a matter of time before indecent exposure ticket number two became a reality. The club was packed, and I had been forced to work the service bar (I should mention that as one of the service bartenders, I was also sharing in a very large pool of gratuities, so it wasn't too hard for me to be "forced" to work it).

As I was just getting into my rhythm behind the bar, one of my bouncers came up to tell me that there was a line of men waiting to get into the men's room, and that one of our lady patrons was sitting in a stall, "servicing" the men who were waiting in line. Now, considering that we had vice cops *everywhere* in the club, and the fact that all of our shows were for ladies only, the only men in the club were my employees; I was more than just a little upset. I reminded my faithful employee that we had the cops in the audience, and that he needed to get his ass into the men's room and take care of the problem. I would be out just as soon as I finished the drink order in front of me.

Not five minutes later, I closed down the service bar and walked over to the men's room, past some of the waiters and bartenders standing in line. I got there just as my bouncer was walking out. "Taken care of boss" was what he told me as he was pulling up his pants...or should I say, ex-bouncer, because I fired him on the spot, and the line of my male employees seemed to disappear as they all rushed back to work. The lovely little angel sitting in the stall looked as if she should be home with her husband and three kids, baking cookies. I allowed her to finish her last "guest," and she just smiled and went back to her table...*and I was handed my second ticket as I left the restroom.*

• • •   • • •   • • •

My general manager, Chuck, and I decided to visit a few of our invited guests, the topless dancers who caused so much commotion over the weekend; *it was the least we could do to say thank you for the first indecent exposure incident.* We pulled up in front of their club in matching Lincoln Continental Mark V's (honest, it was just a coincidence), complete with an attitude and our bar's "change banks" in the trunks of our cars. (We both had a tendency to keep the extra cash in our cars instead of the safe, just in case we got hit with another "keeper" looking for easy cash.)

From the moment we walked into the room, we were treated like royalty; the girls escorted us to two open seats in front of the stage and started what had to be the most impressive "table dance" in the small club's history. There were ten dancers working the floor, and at the start of the next song, four of them were dancing on the stage, directly in front of us. Three more placed chairs on each side of Chuck and me, with one between us, and started dancing on the chairs. The last three dancers in the club were dancing behind us. We were not the only customers in the bar, but we had *all* the dancers. I could totally understand why the rest of the customers were yelling their dissatisfaction, but screw it, we were having a blast.

By the end of the afternoon, we were all having so much fun that six of the ten girls working the day shift decided that we should keep the party going, so they piled into our two cars after their shift was over. We spent the rest of the night, as well as the rest of the money in our trunks, visiting the different bars in the area, eventually ending up at Gatsby's until closing, then back to Chuck's apartment for breakfast. Just Chuck, myself, and six professional dancers... Those lovely ladies remained VIP (very important person) customers of ours for as long as we managed the nightclub, but we did get them to promise never to collect G-strings again.

• • •   • • •   • • •

It was an extremely successful first six months of operation for me. The Chippendales dancers were more popular than ever and my staff were making a lot of money, and having fun doing it. My twenty-fifth birthday was coming up and I was feeling pretty good about myself. July 7, my birthday, started out with my head waitress Jean offering me a "mercy fuck" for my birthday (she was feeling sorry for me not having the time to have any type of relationship); it was going to be a good day. Our regular customers were coming in for our normal Friday happy hour, and our little disc jockey, April, was just starting to play some tunes (April was an adorable little nineteen-year-old who lived for her music). I was sitting on the bar, enjoying a Chivas Regal on the rocks with a Chivas water "back" (it was, after all, my birthday) when Jean showed up carrying a tray of shot glasses.

My customers and staff had decided to help me celebrate, so they bought me a few drinks: twenty-five years old should be celebrated with twenty-five shots of Chivas, with one for luck, and as I was already enjoying the Chivas in front of me, I figured, why not? About the only thing that I can remember, then and now, is that I was crawling on my hands and knees while trying to find the bathroom. I received no help from anyone, but when I finally made it to the employees' lounge, I thought that I was going to die. The "porcelain god" helped, and I was *almost* able to stand when I ventured back out into the bar. Within minutes, Jean was back with another twenty-six shots on her tray. As I lay cowering in the corner of the bar, I really wasn't paying attention when she mentioned that it was just twenty-six shots of watered-down Coca-Cola. Needless to say, I wasn't quite up for the "mercy fuck" that she had offered me earlier.

A Few of Our Regular Customers

David was probably one of the most interesting of my regulars. Approximately sixty years old, he was a portly gentleman who made a lot of stinking money. He would come to the bar every night with his twenty-two-year-old college girlfriend, and would always buy a round for the bar, at least once a night. He was in the temporary employment business; he would sit back for months and sometimes years at a time, waiting for a union strike. Factory workers, school bus drivers, garbage men, it didn't matter who they were; he would be paid large sums of money to supply a temporary workforce during the strike. He would bus them in by the hundreds, pay the laborers minimum wage, and pocket the difference.

As I mentioned, he made a lot of money, but drove around in an old, beat-up Plymouth station wagon (the only clean spot on the car was the area cleaned off by the windshield wipers). He never carried less than $10,000 in cash on any given day, and he shared his $4,000,000 home in the hills with his girlfriend.

David's niece was getting married one Saturday afternoon and he asked me to cater the reception at Gatsby's. It had been scheduled to last only four hours, but as the end drew near, the party started to take on a life of its own. It was getting bigger and louder. David walked over to the band and asked them how much it would take to keep them playing. The lead singer, being a smart ass, called out $100 for fifteen minutes. David handed him $2,000 and told him to keep playing until it ran out. He then came over and handed me $2,000 to spread around with the bartenders. The party lasted until midnight, and David tipped me an additional $2,000 for making it a great party. A few years later, I was told that he had passed away and that his girlfriend had inherited the house in the hills.

• • •   • • •   • • •

"Deli" Jack was an Englishman who owned a little Italian delicatessen in Balboa Peninsula. Many years before I was born, he held the patents for the jet engines used on the 707 and 727 jet airliners, and that was where he made most of his money. The deli was his retirement. He slipped once and shared with me that he had over twelve corporations, and that his annual tax bill was over $2,000,000, but what he was most proud of were the two Rolls-Royce he had parked in the alley behind the deli. I stopped by his deli one day on my way back from the beach, and he invited me to take a ride in one of his cars (he loved to show them off). We left his deli and drove down the Balboa Peninsula, swung over to Balboa Island, and from there, we were going to take the small auto ferry back to the peninsula.

Jack pulled the Rolls onto the ferry, and we settled in for the quick eight-minute ride to the other side, that is, until it came time to pay the attendant. The cost of the ferry was only thirty-five cents, but Jack didn't have any money on him at all, and neither did I (I was still in my swim trunks). There we were, having to backup the Rolls Royce to get off the ferry, because the head of *twelve* corporations and the owner of *two* Rolls Royce and I didn't have thirty-five cents between us.

A few months later, Jack approached me to see if I could help one of his partners with a Nevada gaming license. "Big Al" was trying to open "Big Al's Chicago Style Casino & Speakeasy" in Reno, Nevada, but couldn't get his gaming license approved. I met Big Al at Gatsby's for dinner to explore the possibilities. Big Al walked up to my table, put his twelve-inch cigar on a small dinner plate, and placed a .45 caliber automatic in front of him. Once again, I was thinking that I might be a little out of my league.

The only thing that Al and Jack would have to "fix," to prepare me to be the front man for their next venture, was my net worth. I would need to have a minimum net worth of $5,000,000 before the gaming commission would even consider my application, and for the small price of $5,000, I could rent the net worth from a few friends of Jack's. I had a few pennies stashed away and my ego was only heading higher, so I gave them the money. For the next twelve months, I owned 6,000 acres of a silver mine in Nevada, a 20 percent interest in a gold mine in California, and 5,000 acres of land in Arizona. I now had a net worth of $5,000,000. I wasn't allowed to touch it, or tell anyone I had it, or, God forbid, try to use it or sell it, but I was a multimillionaire on paper for exactly one year. Unfortunately, Big Al couldn't deliver on other promises to his other "partners," and I went back to being a bartender/manager, less the $5,000 I had "invested." *Live and learn.*

•   •   •   •   •   •   •   •   •

Jolene was a short, slightly overweight little girl, about twenty-one years old, who decided that *my* life was a little too boring. She came into the bar six nights a week, and for six nights a week, she would get drunk and make passes at me. I was trying to be nice, but it was getting pretty annoying. I tried very hard to ignore her. I had actually been ignoring all the women who came to the club. It hadn't occurred to me that the more I ignored a beautiful woman, the more attention I seemed to get. I moved in with my girlfriend, Gail, and her daughter a few months earlier, and for the first time in a very long while, I was actually trying to behave. Even Jean, my head waitress, tried to protect me and told Jolene to leave me alone, but nothing seemed to help. That night, Jolene called my house and told my girlfriend that the reason I wasn't coming home before two in the morning every night was because I was at her house, fucking her. When I got home that night, I pulled into my driveway to find every stitch of clothes that I owned thrown across the front lawn—and it was raining. The fact that the bar didn't close until two, that I was normally there at least until three, closing it up and restocking the bar, and the fact that it was *my* house didn't seem to matter to my now ex-girlfriend.

•   •   •   •   •   •   •   •   •

Rachel was a small, exotic, lovely creature who stopped in at Gatsby's twice a week, always during happy hour. I enjoyed her conversation and her attitude, and was always glad to see her when she came in. She had fast become my weekly fantasy, because no matter how hard I tried, I just could not convince her to go out with me (fantasizing about her was still better than nothing). Rachel never had the time for more than one drink, and she was always nice and flirtatious, but she gave me no chance at all to get to know her better. I couldn't stop the fantasies, but it sure would have been nice to make at least *one* of them come true…maybe someday, when I would be a little older, a little wiser, and a lot less arrogant.

• • •   • • •   • • •

Richard was a successful local banker who dreamed of someday owning a bar; Bob and his girlfriend also dreamed of someday owning a bar. The three of them would spend hours asking questions and throwing ideas at me. Whether we agreed or disagreed, it made for some interesting and intense conversations, especially when they would tell me when I was wrong. As I mentioned earlier, *I needed to be a little older, a little wiser, and a lot less arrogant.*

A Few of My Friends
Chris is my friend, as well as a regular customer of mine, since my first days at Hof's Hut. He loved beautiful women, almost as much as I did, and almost as much as he liked gambling. He had been married twice and divorced twice to the same woman, and has two kids; he enjoyed the single life far more than the married life, and he was never really good at hiding that fact. He owned a car leasing company but was technically semiretired—and only leased cars to a select clientele. The majority of his time was spent gambling and visiting topless bars, and the local topless bar of choice? The Mustang, located just a few minutes from Gatsby's Rendezvous.

About once or twice a week, Chris would run by Gatsby's to pick me up on his way to the Mustang. He liked the company, but he also needed me to help him "stay in control." The Mustang is where Chris did most of his car leasing business, as his "select clientele" were the girls dancing in the club. There were ten girls currently leasing cars from Chris, and on the first of each month, he would go in to collect their payments—ten cars at $300 per month, always paid in cash, and the girls never missed a payment. Chris would bring me along to make sure that I stopped him from tipping the girls after they danced (the $3,000 he collected could go a long way in a topless bar...you can make so many new friends).

Chris was probably one of the first recipients of the California handicapped parking permit. He had two bad legs, a crippled hand, and, even on a good day, he wasn't that special in the looks department, but the girls *loved* him. Not only did he make it possible for them to establish credit and lease a new car, but he would also finance the plastic surgery that the girls found so necessary to conduct their business. The bigger the tits, the bigger the tips—and my friend Chris knew this better than anyone.

At least once every few months, Chris would take a liking to a new dancer, lease her a car, pay for her new breasts, and very probably put her into a new apartment for a couple of months. Total investment on his part: zero. The profit he made on the car would more than pay for the breasts and the new apartment, and Chris would be having sex with his "new" client, for as long as it took him to put it all together, normally a two-month process. *I could only hope that my retirement goes as well as his.*

• • •   • • •   • • •

Chris and I decided to celebrate Memorial Day weekend in Las Vegas. He had a friend offer the use of one of his limousines for the weekend, and all it would cost us was the price of the driver. To make the trip just a little more interesting, Chris invited a couple of the dancers from a local topless bar.

Christine and Cathy looked as if they were created from the same mold; both stood at about five feet four inches, both had short, blond hair, both looked as if a strong gust of wind would blow them over…they were dolls.

The limo picked us all up from the Mustang at two in the morning, when the girls finished their shift. We made sure that the car was fully loaded… scotch, bourbon, vodka, gin, and champagne, two bottles each. As we entered the entrance to the freeway, we opened the champagne, and twenty minutes later, the second bottle; in the five hours it took us to reach Las Vegas, the only alcohol left was a half bottle of bourbon, not bad for only four of us.

As we entered the lobby of the Golden Nugget Hotel, Christine slipped at the entrance to the stairs, fell, and passed out on the marble floor of the lobby; Chris was being held up by one of the columns by the lobby entrance and one of the doormen. I walked up to the front desk to check us all in, then Cathy announced to anyone interested, "They're going to be freakin' pissed, 'cause I ain't putting out."

I checked us all in and we went up to our rooms; Chris and I in one room, Christine and Cathy in the next, and our chauffeur next to them. I was in Vegas, wide awake and ready to play; all I needed was my bags to be delivered to the room so that I could get cleaned up and hit the casino. Twenty minutes and no bags, so I called down to the front desk and was told that they were already on their way, but after another twenty minutes, still no bags. When I called back to the desk, I was told that they had been delivered to the girls' room, but when I tried to call them, all I got was a busy signal. I knocked on their door with no results, and then tried to call again, with the same results. All I wanted were my bags. If they were on the phone, why weren't they answering the door? I called housekeeping to let me in, but the dead bolt was in place and they couldn't open the door. They called maintenance and they couldn't get in, and finally, we called security… all with the same results.

Over an hour had passed of knocking on the door and calling the room, when security finally authorized the maintenance department to take the door apart. Another thirty minutes passed when the maintenance people removed the door frame and started to lift the door out. That's when Cathy decided to peek through the opening.

"This is security. Open the door, now!"

The phone had been knocked off the receiver when the girls literally passed out on the floor. They hadn't even made it to the bed. *This was going to be a really interesting trip.*

It was six at night, and we were rested, cleaned up, and ready to hit the town. Our first stop was the first roulette table we came to. Cathy and Chris decided that it wasn't their game, so they were just going to watch Christine and me. With every roll of the ball came a win for either Christine or me, or both of us; we couldn't lose. It was getting very exciting; the chips were piling up faster than we could count them, but when Christine leaned over to me, it was all about to change. "Joe," she whispered, "the asshole next to me is stealing my chips."

I looked over, and just as I was about to stand up, a security guard put his hands on my shoulder and said, "No worries. We have it handled." And when I looked around, there were actually four security guards surrounding the table.

The guards took the thief next to us, and his wife, into custody and immediately returned Christine's chips. We had been having so much fun winning that I wasn't paying any attention to the crowd around us. I had thought that it was because we had been winning so much, or at the very least, the crowd was watching Christine in her micromini, and the fact that she had forgotten her underwear, or maybe it was the tube top that couldn't contain her "D" cups. *But I was a little too busy to care about a couple of chips.*

Just a few minutes after that, Cathy asked Chris if there were any "hookers" in the area. She had never seen one and was curious. Chris looked around for *almost* a minute and picked out a small blond sitting at the bar and told Cathy. Christine immediately jumped up and screamed far louder than she should have, "A hooker? Where?" And just a few minutes after that, our chauffeur asked me if I could advance him the tip that he was hoping to receive *now*, because he was broke and had lost the money I had already paid him for his services, *and we had only been awake for about an hour.*

· · · · · · · · ·

After what seemed like forever, the girls finally left us to go to bed, and Chris and I stayed downstairs, at one of the smaller bars, to enjoy a quiet drink— *without* the constant ramblings of our escorts. Over all, it hadn't been a bad trip. Chris and I made some money, and the girls were actually fun to be with when they weren't drinking too much.

We were sitting at a small, isolated bar next to the casino floor when the bartender came over to ask if we would like another drink. I responded, "Please, and could we buy one for that lovely woman across the bar as well?" When he complied, she immediately picked up her drink and came over to thank us. She wasn't shy, and within a few moments, she asked if I would be interested. "In what?" I asked (I wasn't always the sharpest tool in the shed when it came to recognizing a "professional").

"Me," she replied. "It will only cost you $100."

I gracefully declined her offer and looked over at Chris to see if he was interested; he *was* thinking about it, but he declined as well (he probably thought that he still had a shot with the girls upstairs). We had a pretty good run at blackjack, so I turned to the lovely young woman and handed her a $100 bill. "Here you go. Just tell your friends that you got it talking to a couple of nice guys at the bar, with no strings attached."

She immediately picked up the $100 bill and, with both of us in tow, walked over to the closest blackjack table to make a bet. She placed the bill on the table, looked at the dealer, and said, "Money plays." The cards were dealt, two tens for her, a nineteen for the dealer; after he paid her, she just looked up and left the $200 on the table for the next bet. She hit again...and again, and again. In less time than it took me to go to the bathroom, she was playing $1,000 a hand and couldn't seem to lose. She handed me three hundred-dollar chips to say thank you for getting her started. This was way out of my comfort zone. I'm good for $25 to $100 bets, but anything more than that makes me very nervous. Yet our new companion kept winning. Chris was trying to keep up with her, but I had enough and was happy with the extra $300. *Our companion had close to $30,000 in front of her.*

I decided to take a break and went up to my room, undressed, and stepped into the shower. All I could think about was our lovely professional, with over $30,000 that I was essentially responsible for. The least she could have done was offer me a massage, a blow job, *something*. After all, she was a "professional." Not five minutes later, the shower door opened, and there she stood, looking even better now that I thought she was going to join me in the shower. But all she wanted was *her* $300 back. She had lost everything she had won. Apparently, my friend Chris had no problem bringing her up to our room.

In the morning, I made some calls. I couldn't wait to tell my friends that I had "financed a hooker" "hooked" on gambling.

•   •   •   •   •   •   •   •   •

Our last dinner together before we were to leave was the most pleasant, primarily because we were all sober. Cathy looked over at us and said, "You know, I really had a good time. Thank you."

I looked back and replied, "Cathy, that's all Chris and I had ever asked of you." But then, they started drinking again. By the time we piled into the limo for the ride home, I had had enough. I asked the driver to pull over. I picked up a blanket and pillow, and moved to the front seat next to the driver. It was much safer with him than in the back with the girls, and a hell of a lot quieter. I needed some rest.

· · · · · · · · ·

Gatsby's Rendezvous was successful by anyone's standards; that's why it was so upsetting when I got the call…the restaurant was on fire. At first, I thought it was a joke and that the caller was just telling me how "hot" the club had become. But according to the fire marshal, it was an accidental fire, which started in twenty-one places…simultaneously. *Apparently, when you piss off the wrong "partners," there are repercussions.*

I was on the street, looking for work, and my first phone call was to my friend Joe…*still working at Lorenzo's.*

· · · · · · · · ·

Several years later, I had heard that my little darling disc jockey, April, was aggressively buying Orange County real estate and paying cash. Apparently, she had followed her dream of a music career to Las Vegas and found out that she could make much more money doing $1,000 a night tricks on the strip. It was 1976, and $1,000 was considered a lot of money. What on earth could she possibly be doing to earn $1,000 in one night?

I was waiting in line to get past the pearly gates, but apparently, I had to get passed Saint Peter first. An imposing sight, a solidly built man, with white hair and a long, flowing white beard, he was asking questions of the man in front of me.

"Have you ever cheated on your tax returns?"

"Never, Sir," answered the man. "Thirty years and I always paid what I was asked."

"Have you ever used foul language or taken the name of the Lord in vain?"

"No, Sir, never."

"Have you ever cheated on your wife?"

"No, Sir, not in twenty years of marriage."

"Okay, you can pass."

I stepped up and Saint Peter looked down at me, then said, "Have you ever cheated on your tax returns?"

"Of course," I replied. "Everyone does. Why should I give those political bastards a dime of my money?"

"Have you ever used foul language or taken the Lord's name in vain?"

"Goddamn it, of course, whenever I fucking had to."

"Have you ever cheated on your wife?"

"Fucking A. That's how I got into this mess. I came across this bitch walking along the street. I asked her into my car and drove off. The bitch was amazing. She had great technique and was giving me one hell of a blow job, but when I came, I lost control of the car...and here I am."

Saint Peter told me to go stand off to the side, and that he would be with me in a moment. Three hours later, he came up to me and asked, "Are you ready?"

"Saint Peter, now wait a minute. You know those other guys were freaking lying. Why am I the only one getting punished? I, at least, told the truth."

*"You're not getting punished, my Son, for being so honest. I'm taking you back down. I want you to introduce me to that **lovely woman** with the great technique."*

Rooney's

· · ·   · · ·   · · ·

Bob Rooney and his wife arrived in Southern California with only one purpose on their minds: to own a restaurant and nightclub. Together with their good friend and partner, Dick, who had over twenty years' experience in the business, and the money they received from the sale of their two florist shops, they were determined to buy a successful operation and make it better.

Lorenzo's in the city of Orange was a very successful restaurant for over ten years, but unfortunately, a very nasty divorce was forcing the owner to liquidate all of his holdings at "fire sale" prices. Bob Rooney's timing could not have been better.

When I met with Bob and Dick for my initial interview, I was in a pretty good position. I had been fortunate to have worked the bar a few years earlier and I knew the bar, the regulars, and the staff. My training requirements would be minimal, and it didn't hurt that my good friend Joe P. was still there and wanted me back on the day shift.

The location of the restaurant was good for both the business crowd during the day as well as the dinner crowd at night. Our chef had been there for years and we had a great reputation for serving excellent food at a reasonable price. The live entertainment was good and we could always rely on the band to fill the bar at night. We had good food, good entertainment, and some of the best bartenders and servers in the area. We weren't too worried about the change in ownership. *How much damage could a florist do?*

After only two months in operation, the name changed from Lorenzo's to Rooney's. The general manager and partner, Dick, was asked to leave due to irreconcilable differences on how to run a restaurant...and the florist took over.

• • •   • • •   • • •

Katie was a doll, tiny, very petite, with just two obvious exceptions—big, round eyes and big, round tits, and she was so damn adorable. She was also my cocktail waitress *and* my girlfriend. She rode a bicycle to work every day, primarily because at twenty-four years of age, she had never taken the time to apply for a driver's license; she had always been just too busy. On the days when I wasn't driving, she would ride up to the restaurant wearing just a halter top, shorts, and flip-flops, but she would always carry her uniform and a change of clothes in her bag (just in case we were going to go out after our shifts were over). We had been seeing each other for a few months and were having a great time. We worked together and played together, but we gave each other enough space so as not to be a burden. Our only challenge occurred when Bob decided, in his infinite wisdom, to increase our schedule and open for Sunday brunch. He thought it would be a great idea if we opened two hours earlier than any of our competition. Hell, by the time he was finished, we were opening two hours earlier than even some of the churches in the area.

Katie and I both worked the Saturday-night closing shift, and by the time we finished our side work and restocked the bar, it was usually at around three-thirty in the morning before we got home. Bob wanted the restaurant to be open at nine in the morning for Sunday brunch, which meant that we would have to be there by eight. We might be able to squeeze in about four hours' sleep, *but God forbid if we actually wanted a cup of coffee or felt like having a sex life.*

Our little shot at defiance came when we realized that the only other employee in the restaurant who came in that early was our sous chef, and he *never* came out of his kitchen. We could count on being alone in the dining room and bar for at least two hours every morning. We got into the habit of going right to sleep when we got off work the night before, so that we would be rested and ready for a little fun when we got to the restaurant in the morning. Katie would leave for work wearing her sheer nightgown covered by a short robe, and I would throw on a long robe to cover my briefs, and that was it (between the trunk of my car and her oversized bag, we both carried our uniforms and a change of clothes).

We decided to "mark our territory," so to speak, and we took great strides in leaving "our mark" on as many parts of the restaurant as we could. We developed new positions (for us), and had sex in the liquor room, behind the bar, on top of the bar, in the restrooms (both of them), on the stage, in the foyer, and against several walls; we gave new meaning to the term Sunday brunch.

• • •   • • •   • • •

Pouring cost (PC), a bartender's dilemma; over-pour to keep a customer happy and under-pour (also known as a "short" pour) to keep the owner happy. A "pouring cost" of between eighteen and twenty-four will normally keep the owner happy. Anything over that and they'll think that the bartender is either giving away too much alcohol or they're stealing. Joe P. and I loved to keep our regular customers very happy at Rooney's, but to take care of them in the style that they have become accustomed to, we needed to make some adjustments to our PC. We would have to short pour some of our drink orders to offset the over-pour for our regular customers.

During our lunch rush, the most popular drink was also the easiest to work with, our Bloody Mary. Joe P. had created our own Bloody Mary mix, and because it was so tasty and so good, no one would miss a little less alcohol. Before we opened our doors, I would set up thirty glasses, salt the rims, and fill each one halfway with our special Bloody Mary mix. I then picked up a vodka bottle and quickly skimmed it across the top of all thirty glasses. Maybe four ounces of vodka made it into the glasses...*four ounces for all thirty glasses*. As the drinks were ordered, the only thing left for me to do was add ice and hand them to the servers. Not once in the entire time that I worked there did anyone send a Bloody Mary back or complain that there wasn't enough alcohol.

Next was our happy hour martini crowd. We would fill a bottle about three-quarters full of either gin or vodka and then fill it with water. They were stored in the refrigerator until such time when someone would order a martini "up," then all we would have to do was pour it into a chilled martini glass—no mix, no fuss, and our customers loved them.

The evening crowd enjoyed our margaritas, and as I watched Joe make them, it would be extremely rare when he would even *pick up* a tequila bottle. Every so often, an occasional customer might ask for some "extra" tequila, then Joe would make a big show at "over-pouring." We have our ways, and in those rare moments, the "extra" over-pouring meant that the drink had about an ounce of tequila, no more.

Although this may seem to be unethical for some, we felt that part of our jobs as professional bartenders was to keep everyone happy, not just a select few. Our "over-pour" recipients, our regulars, felt that they were special and never complained, and our "short" pour recipients loved our drinks, always had a great time, they never complained, and they *never* had a hangover. Good atmosphere, good company, great service, and satisfied customers were the result. You would be surprised at how often a customer would act as if they had too much to drink just because of their surroundings, and the amount of alcohol they *thought* they had consumed. All felt special, all would come back for more, and our PC was never more than fourteen, *which meant our owner never complained.*

As I realized much later, these little tricks are never acceptable. You are essentially ripping off good customers and giving a disservice to the regulars.

· · · · · · · ·

Our nightly entertainment was a combination of soft listening music during the dinner hours and hard core rock and roll from ten to closing. It was the perfect accompaniment to the décor and style of the restaurant. It had been a couple of hours since my shift had ended and I was still sitting at the bar, when Bob asked me to hang around in case Joe P. needed some help. He was expecting a busy night.

The band had just arrived and was starting to set up their instruments, the dining room was full with a thirty-minute wait for a table, and the happy hour crowd in the lounge just didn't seem like they wanted to leave. It was already a very good night. I looked around and took stock as to what was going on around me; Joe P. was at the top of his game.

No one in the room was without a drink. The drink orders coming in from the dining room were being made as fast as they were being ordered, and Joe had the bar in stitches. He was picking on one of the band members and it seemed to put everyone in a good mood, including the band member. Joe had a very good handle on what was going on around him; he was keeping track of his *entire* surroundings. I was just about to say good night to all when April walked into the bar.

April was one of those "married" women whom every "single" man wanted. She was extremely exotic, sensual, and had the look that all men, and more than a few women, would fantasize about. But she was *very* married. Her husband would accompany her into the bar at least once a week, just to show her off to the rest of the world. Joe and I were just two of the many who would have to wipe the drool off our chins every time she would walk into the room. She was always amazing to watch, but this time was different. She was alone, with no sign of her husband anywhere, and she had a *very* determined look on her face as she approached the bar.

As was always the case, whenever she arrived, the room gave pause, out of respect, just to give her a moment to pass. She was that stunningly beautiful. She went straight to the bar, stood directly in front of my friend Joe, and announced that she had just walked into her home to find her "perfect" husband fucking her "perfect" best friend on her kitchen table.

She looked straight into Joe's eyes and simply said, "I'll only ask this once: outside in five minutes. I need a place to stay for the night." Now Joe P. can be called many things, but stupid wasn't one of them. Without any hesitation (it must have been one of those "as fast as he had to be" moments), he walked over to the end of the bar, turned on all of the overhead lights, and announced, "Last call." The room was packed, and it was only eight-thirty. As he leaped over the bar, he threw me the keys to the register and told me to lock up, and then he was gone, out the door, and into April's car in less than two minutes, a record even by his standards.

When I was finally able to close my mouth, I slid back behind the bar, lowered the lights, rearranged the bottles in the well, and finished Joe's shift. Damn, I was jealous. Joe probably hadn't given any thought at all to whether this was going to cost him his job or not, and he honestly wouldn't have cared. He was thinking with his "little" head and had much more important things on his mind. Besides, somewhere in the back of his mind (the "big" head), he knew I would cover for him.

Joe and I were the only two bartenders on Bob's payroll, and quite frankly, he would never risk losing either of us as long as we didn't cost him money. Bob's reputation as a restaurateur was still subject to speculation, and Joe and I were a very good team. We worked well together but didn't compete with each other, and on those days when one of us would disappear, either getting drunk or getting laid, the other would always cover the shift, no questions asked, with no complaints. Usually, Joe and I were responsible for our own schedules, the liquor ordering, and the shift changes, so Bob wouldn't give this a second thought, *except for the fact that he was probably just as jealous as I was.*

● ● ● ● ● ● ● ● ●

I would normally close the bar at two in the morning and then stop off at a local coffee shop for a little breakfast and some "downtime," usually making it to my apartment at around four. I felt like I had just closed my eyes when I was jarred awake by the doorbell. A quick glance at the digital clock radio next to my bed confirmed that there really were *two* seven o'clocks in a twenty-four-hour day. (Bartenders have a tendency to forget that when they are working until two in the morning.)

With almost three hours of sleep, I draped a towel around my naked butt and went downstairs to answer the door. The morning sun was blinding, but I did manage to notice a very cute, little brunette standing in front of me. She was trying to convince me to buy some magazine subscriptions, but the sun was too intense, so I invited her into my apartment to finish her sales pitch. She was a junior at a local community college and was selling magazine subscriptions for their college fund-raiser.

She immediately made herself comfortable at the kitchen table and I offered her coffee…or a shot of tequila and a beer (the only choices that seemed to make any sense at seven in the morning). She chose the latter and spread her magazine options all over the table. With every shot of tequila came a magazine subscription. After almost an hour and nine shots later, I was going to be the proud recipient of nine magazine subscriptions. To celebrate her great sales technique, she grabbed my towel and ran up to my bedroom, shedding her clothes along the way. *Oh, the things we tend to do to celebrate higher education.*

We came up for air at around eleven, and I was feeling so good about investing in the local college fund that I thought it would be a great idea to take my new companion to Las Vegas for dinner. We were showered, in the car, and on our way in what seemed like minutes.

From my apartment to downtown Las Vegas is a four-hour trip—and we needed *all* of it just to sober up. She slept while I drove, but by the time we finished checking in to the Golden Nugget Hotel, we were ready for round two. Another couple of hours in bed and another shower, and we hit the casino.

She started my day at seven in the morning, and in the next eight hours, we got drunk, we had sex twice, and wound up in Las Vegas. By *any* bartender's standard, not a bad day, but in the eight hours that we were together, the only real conversation we had was about the magazines she sold me. It became painfully obvious that there wasn't anything of value between those tiny little ears. *She was cute, she was fun, but she wasn't the sharpest tool in the shed.* After a quick dinner, I checked us out of the hotel and had us back at my apartment by seven—one *hell* of a twenty-four-hour day.

I never saw her again, but I had nine magazines delivered to me every month for the next three years, and except for the TV *Guide*, the other eight (whatever they were) never made it out of their wrappers. *Nine magazines for three years: $285. The trip to Vegas: breakeven. Twenty-four hours in support of higher education? Priceless.*

• • • • • • • •

The Stadium was a nice little restaurant across the street from Angel Stadium. It had just been sold to an investment firm and I was asked to give my "professional" opinion about the qualifications of the current management team (I was starting to establish a reputation for having more to offer than just being behind the bar).

The actual lounge was dominated by a large, rectangular bar in the middle of the room. It had three bartender stations and ample liquor storage, both on the center island behind the bar and in the overhead shelves above each well. After meeting with both the general manager and his bar manager, I had only three questions: How much liquor is stocked in the bar? How much did it cost? And are there any inventory controls in place? Reasonable questions that every bar manager should know, and every general manager should check *every month.*

After the general manager voiced his opinion on how ridiculous that was, the bar manager jumped in to say something derogatory about my family background and that no one had the ability to have that information available at a moment's notice. They were going to need to take a complete inventory to get my answers and that maybe I should check back in a couple of days.

I needed to make a point, so, with the owner's permission, I spent five minutes behind the bar, mentally taking note of how many liquor bottles there were, and then another five minutes walking around the bar, counting the bottles stored on the open shelves overhead. I then mentally calculated the number of bottles, multiplied by the average cost of one bottle of liquor (a number I received from the liquor salesman on the account), and came up with 232 bottles at a cost of $2,860.

As the bar manager's snickering and laughter subsided, I made a deal. If I were wrong, no problem; I would leave and tell the new owners that they would be able to handle the job. But if I were right? They would leave. I asked the general manager to take a quick inventory and pull the liquor invoices, and two hours later, they realized that there were, in fact, 234 bottles of liquor, at a cost of $2,805.

A little simple math and more than a little luck…but the general manager received an education and the incompetent bar manager was gone by the end of the day. My compensation was an open bar tab for two months, one that I used quite often, and another addition to my resume. *This business is tough enough…we shouldn't have to deal with bigotry and ignorance.*

A Few of Our Regular Customers

Ron, one of our regular customers, told me that his son was about to open a bartending school in Anaheim. He had heard that I had turned down an offer to be one of their instructors, but he would like for me to reconsider (Ron was also an investor and he would feel more comfortable if I could help, at least at the beginning). I agreed, but imagine my amazement when I discovered that Ron's son had just graduated from an eight-week crash course from another bartending school, and had spent the last two weeks as a part-time catering bartender for one of the local hotels.

How he convinced his dad to invest in this, I'll never know, but even a father's love has to be tempered with a little common sense. I knew then why

Ron asked me to reconsider. How could his son possibly teach something that he hasn't learned himself? Ron was worried that his twenty-two-year-old son—with only two weeks of part-time work and an eight-week crash course—might not have enough experience to protect his investment. *You think?* I spent the next six months as one of their instructors. A few extra dollars, Ron was happy, and it was great for my ego and resume.

• • •   • • •   • • •

Curt and Jean were still here. They were regular customers when it was called Lorenzo's, and they had survived the change in ownership. It was always an extreme pleasure to serve them, and we spent many Mondays together, as we did years earlier, sampling the strange and exotic liquors hidden in the back bar.

• • •   • • •   • • •

Richard, Bob, and his girlfriend, Cathy, had followed me from Gatsby's Rendezvous to Rooney's; the location changed, but not the conversation. We were still spending hours every day talking about owning and operating a bar, but what made the conversations interesting was that with the different locations, there were different points of view. Gatsby's Rendezvous was a large nightclub with a dining room, but the emphasis had always been on the nightclub. Rooney's was a restaurant that served lunch and dinner, and had a lounge, but even though the lounge offered nightly entertainment, the emphasis would always be on the food. Two completely different operations had my little trio of future restaurateurs so very confused. It was always a pleasure to see them and I totally enjoyed the conversations.

A Few of My Friends

Steve is a computer software genius and, without a doubt, one of the craziest people I've ever met. Depending on his mood, he could show up driving his BMW convertible, wearing a custom-made three-piece silk suit, or pull up on his Harley Davidson motorcycle clad in his "leathers." But regardless of what he was wearing, *he was still crazy.*

I first met Steve while I was attempting to get a drink at a local restaurant called Chicago Joe's, a great place, but it was Pam the bartender who made it special. Over the years, Pam had become one of my "go-to" bartender friends. I would go to her with my relationship problems, go to her with my customer problems, and go to her with my work problems. We all need that special someone to talk to...*and she was mine.*

Steve was standing in the middle of the waitress station, directly in front of Pam, effectively blocking me from ordering *my* drink, and I was getting pissed. He was dressed in a business suit, but I noticed a tiny braid tucked under his jacket, so I told him to get the hell out of the way or I'd cut it off. It wasn't exactly one of my more diplomatic moments, but I was really thirsty and patience never was one of my strong points. When he turned around, I thought I was looking at the younger brother I never had. We were instant friends. Pam formally introduced us and, without too much encouragement, we were both standing in the waitress station, pissing off the rest of the customers.

● ● ● ● ● ● ● ● ●

Steve asked me to join him and his girlfriend, Diane, for a drink at *the* new club in town, "Players," a fancy affair with an extremely large, rectangular bar and a reputation for being the new meeting place for the wannabe "players" in the area. It had been open for only a couple of weeks, but the place was very crowded, with standing room only (when they coined the phrase, "packed like sardines," this must have been what they were thinking of).

I pushed my way into the place, and when I finally located Steve, he was pushed up against the bar in front of one of the bartender stations, but Diane was nowhere to be found. It was three deep at the bar, and the five bartenders working couldn't pour drinks fast enough. Their heads were buried in the ice. As I moved next to him, I ordered my drink and asked when Diane was going to get there. He just mumbled, "She's here."

As I made myself comfortable, I looked around, trying to find her. When I glanced over at Steve, he had this really stupid look on his face and his eyes were slightly glazed. I wasn't quite sure if he was on drugs or just had too much to drink. My first drink went down pretty fast, but I noticed that Steve hadn't touched any of his, and he still had that stupid look on his face. He nodded slightly to the top of the bar, but I was too busy trying to order another drink and didn't give it much notice.

It was actually getting busier and I had no idea how they could squeeze any more people into the place, but customers kept coming in. As we were being pushed even closer against the bar, I finally realized what Steve was attempting to tell me with his nod. Diane was kneeling under the bar counter, in front of Steve, with a part of his anatomy in her mouth. But it was so crowded that no one had any idea what was going on. It was five o'clock in the afternoon and there had to be a couple of hundred customers in the bar, and here was my friend Steve, getting "head" from his girlfriend. After she was finished, Diane stood up between us, and the bartender casually looked over and said, "Welcome back." *I guess I wasn't the only one who noticed.*

Steve always seemed to bring out the best in a woman. It must have been the "bad boy" attitude that he exuded. As I started my shift, I found Steve and his new friend, Caren, sitting at the bar, but after a few moments, they excused themselves. I started to get busy and I didn't notice when they got back. But a few minutes later, they left again. In the first two hours of my shift, Steve and Caren disappeared three times. And every time they got back, Steve had this "shit-eating" grin on his face. "Dude, you've got to spend some time with her," "Dude, you really need to walk her out to her car," "Dude..."

"Enough, Steve. I'm trying to work here."

With Steve's insistence, I finally agreed to connect with Caren the next day to take her shopping. She was new in town and was going to be starting a new career in banking, so I thought she should have something new to wear on her first day. She would feel better about herself and it would help make a really good impression. I picked her up at around two o'clock on Saturday afternoon and headed over to the local mall.

First stop, the lingerie department, where I picked out a few items and Caren took them over to a dressing room. A few minutes later, she walked out, wearing what I had picked out. *Huge mistake.* The negligee she chose to wear *into* the showroom floor was shear, and I could see *everything*. And, unfortunately, I found absolutely *nothing* attractive about her almost naked body. She was *slightly* flabby, *slightly* overweight, and not even close to being even *slightly* athletic. *Amazing how the right clothes can make someone look so damn different.*

I quickly bought the negligee and moved on to business attire in an attempt to cover her up, and then the shoe department. As much as I have always enjoyed the process of buying a woman shoes, I quickly purchased the first pair that she tried on and ushered her out to the car. She was going to look good on her first day on the job, *but I just couldn't get her almost naked, flabby body out of my mind.*

On the way back to her apartment, she asked me to pull over, and as the car rolled to a stop on a quiet section of the road, she unzipped my pants, lowered her head, and the rest is history. In the next two hours, I came four times...and her lips *never* left my dick. For only the second time in my life, I received oral sex from a woman who truly *loved* what she was doing...and now I understood why Steve and Caren kept leaving my bar the night before.

For the next week, Caren wanted more, but I just couldn't. She made reservations at a local hotel for the weekend, she tried to take me to dinner, and she was always hanging out until my shift was over, but I just couldn't get past the way her body looked without clothes. *If only I hadn't seen her naked.*

. . .   .

I had just ended my shift and was standing with Joe P. when she walked back into my life. RC was still beautiful, still impressive, and she had four, very sexy, scantily clad women with her. *Talk about making an impression.*

She had just been made the general manager of the topless bar down the street, and thought it a perfect opportunity to promote the bar and to celebrate. Not exactly the same as when we rolled through Balboa Peninsula to promote Gatsby's Rendezvous, but pretty damn impressive just the same. *RC and I visited each other often, sharing ideas and customers.*

. . .   .

We called him Rock, an old friend and customer of ours, who was owner of a local tire shop. In addition to being one of our better customers, he was also dating one of our waitresses, a big girl named Jackie. Rock liked his women big; the bigger the better. Jackie was taking some time off from work to recover from an intestinal bypass surgery, but by the time the swelling went down, she would *still* be more than 300 pounds.

The restaurant was going to be closed for a three-day weekend, so Joe and I decided to spend it in Vegas. When Rock heard about our trip, he invited himself along (Jackie was going to be out of commission for at least another week and he needed some time away). I wanted to pull into Vegas in time for breakfast, so we left very early the next morning.

We had been on the road for almost three hours and Rock wouldn't shut up; he was on a roll.

"You guys better get me laid," "I better make me some money," "You bastards better take care of me," "I better not lose," "You boys better make sure that I get laid, or I'm going to take you both in the ass," for four solid hours.

Now, both Joe and I are not into men, and the thought of Rock even in the same room with me after that last statement started to worry me; Rock not only loves very big women, he is a very big man, and I was more than just a little concerned. We were only about thirty minutes from the California/Nevada border when I drove over a small hill and got hit with a very bright rising sun, and I had forgotten my sunglasses. Rock was still on a roll, and I was almost getting used to his off-the-wall comments when he went off again: "You bastards, I was with an almost new girlfriend last week who was sooooo big that by the time I got past the first three inches of fat and two inches of pubic hair, I ran out of dick."

Now, I was still blinded by the rising sun when the visual of Rock belly surfing with a very large woman and running out of dick hit me. I started laughing so hard that I started crying; between the sun and my tears, I was truly blind. I can honestly say that I have no recollection of the next twenty miles. Thank God that the car knew what direction we were headed and the speed bumps between the lanes kept me on track. The ride to Vegas and listening to Rock, nonstop for the whole trip, had taken a lot out of me, and when we checked in to the rooms at the Golden Nugget, I made sure we all had different rooms. *I wasn't going to take any chances.*

Minutes after checking in to our rooms, Joe took off; he had slept the whole trip and was ready to have some fun. The first stop was that great game of skill, the Big Spin, usually found at the entrance to every casino. Joe put a $20 bill on the highest odds on the table (20 to 1), and hit. Four hundred dollars was a great start for the weekend, and that was when he disappeared. Rock and I tried to find him over the next two days, but all we got for our trouble were rumors. Joe apparently joined a couple of indigent gentlemen who he found sleeping in the alley next to the Golden Nugget Hotel, and the three of them started on a pretty impressive bar hopping trip through downtown Las Vegas. *I started thinking that maybe he felt it safer than spending time with Rock.*

By the morning of the third day, I was starting to panic. Neither Rock nor I had seen Joe from the moment he won the $400 on the Big Spin. I tried hotel security, the local hospitals, the sheriff's department, the casino staff; no sign of Joe P., and it was time for us to leave. Rock and I checked out of the hotel and went outside to wait for the valet to deliver my car. As it pulled up, we loaded our bags into the trunk, and I looked over at Rock and told him that I would be right back.

On a hunch, I went back up the elevator and knocked on Joe's door. It was opened by hotel security, and there was my friend, passed out, face down on the bed. A couple of Las Vegas's finest and the hotel security guard had found Joe sleeping in the alley with his now very close, new best friends. After a quick search, they found Joe's room key and said, "This one is ours," and brought him back to his room. It was sheer luck that I found him. I picked him up, checked him out of the hotel, and poured him into the backseat of my car.

As I was pulling out of the hotel driveway, Joe opened the car door and leaned out to spit. When his nose bounced off the pavement, he rolled back into the car and passed out again. Four hours later, he woke up with a bloody nose and asked when we would be leaving. I had already dropped Rock off at his house and was just pulling into Joe's driveway. Not one of our best trips to Vegas, but definitely one that I would never forget.

• • •   • • •   • • •

Bob was finally starting to settle down, and he was operating his restaurant as a business, not as fuel for his personal ego. To me, the customers were always the same and very predictable. The entertainment was good, but had been there for years, and the menu hadn't changed for a very long time. Rooney's was no longer a challenge for me and I was feeling like I didn't want to be there from the minute I walked through the door.

Most of my customers saw my dissatisfaction, but three of them decided to offer me an alternative. Several months ago, my little trio of future restaurateurs had invested in a liquor license lottery offered by the California Alcohol Beverage Control Board, and as fortune would have it, they won. They had spent the last few weeks looking at several locations and would like my help with choosing the right one. They were almost there...they had a plan, a new liquor license, money, *and now, a new partner. Hopefully, this will work out a little better than the last time.*

• • •   • • •   • • •

Joe decided that part of my training should include a better appreciation for country music, and there was no better place to start my education than The Cowboy. An extremely large place that included four bars, located on three different levels, and a five-thousand-square-foot dance floor. The place was massive, and as we approached the front door, the line of customers waiting to get in, at $20 a piece, stretched around the building.

We had come to know the two owners quite well: Robert, the operating partner, and Sam, the silent investor. We had no problem walking past the line, and our first stop—and last—was the office. It had been our intention to just stop by to say thank you for letting us in, but both looked up and asked us to sit for a minute.

Robert was in the process of dividing the money they had taken in from the door charges:

"One for me, one for you, one for the IRS (Internal Revenue Service)."

"One. Two for me, two for you, two for the IRS."

"One. Two. Three for me, three for you, fuck the IRS."

"One. Two. Three. Four for me, four for you...IRS who?"

So it went until over $40,000 was distributed, and there were *still* several hundred people waiting in line to get in. They picked up their money, grabbed Joe and me, and we proceeded to the topless bar across the street, RC's place. It's simply amazing how much fun a man can have in a bar employing semi-naked beautiful women, at least when the general manager of the club likes you, and the girls working knew we had $40,000 to play with. So much for getting better acquainted with country music.

Les entered the restroom and walked up to an empty urinal. He casually glanced over at the little man next to him and gasped, "My God, your dick is huge."

*The little gentlemen smiled and, in a soft Irish brogue, told Les, "Well, Laddie, one of the many benefits it is of being a **leprechaun**."*

*The little Irish gentleman gave pause, and then informed Les that if he would let him **have his way** with him, with a simple wave of his magic wand, Les could have one even bigger.*

*A few seconds later, they both entered into a neighboring stall. As Les dropped his pants and leaned forward, the leprechaun **drove it home**. Les squealed, from both the embarrassment and the pain, but the leprechaun just kept pounding away.*

Tears began streaming down his cheeks and the pain was getting worse, when the Irishman asked, "Not to be rude, but how old are you?"

In between the thrusts, Les managed a whimper and a pitiful, "Thirty-two."

"And you still believe in leprechauns?"

The 770 Lounge

. . .   .

When we arrived at the Satin Lounge, it wasn't early, but we were the only customers in the room. It was a small neighborhood beer bar, with a long, straight bar against one wall, a shuffle board game against the opposite wall, and that was it, no tables or chairs, just the bar, the shuffle board, and one employee. She was dressed in a red and white polka dot bikini; she was also the owner, chief cook, and bottle washer...and she looked as tired as the dated bikini.

The Satin Lounge was small, but affordable. It was located at 770 Brea Boulevard, and when we realized that the building had two empty suites adjacent to it, my new partners started to have "visions of grandeur" and negotiated for all three. My job for the next four months, before actually becoming their partner and lead bartender, was to be the general contractor and build it. The new 770 Lounge would keep the existing bar in place, but I would create a small kitchen, a dining room for sixty, and build a piano bar and dance floor in the center of the now expanded room. When completed, I would trade my contractor's hat for bar manager. My future was looking pretty good. After my return from Vietnam, bartender to bar owner in just eight years, and it hadn't cost me a dime of my own money. Damn, *I sure was naïve*.

Our construction was scheduled to last for four months, and I decided that one of my first acts as the managing partner was to hire our lead waitress and two servers *immediately*. Their function during the time we were under construction was to promote the lounge, and for the next eight weeks, Tuesdays through Sundays, I paid them a salary to put on their best bikinis and lay out in the sun to work on their tan. To get the most "exposure," I set them up directly in front of the bar during construction, on the sidewalk, facing the main street. Their pictures hit the local newspaper by the first weekend and the traffic always slowed in front of the bar, just long enough for the girls to pass out our new business cards. I was feeling pretty confident that our grand opening was going to be a huge success.

The type of liquor license we had won in the state lottery had one major restriction: the restaurant had to be open within twelve months from the date of the lottery. We were on a pretty tight schedule. The bar had to be to be open by July 11 or we would lose the license and be out of business before we started. I was managing a construction crew of five, but it was hard physical labor with very long hours. Often, we would work through the night, break for breakfast, and then right back at it.

For the first time in a very long time, my weight dropped to 185 pounds (the last time I had seen that was when it was on the way up, somewhere around age fifteen). The combination of no drinking and hard physical labor for four months resulted in my losing thirty-five pounds, and more importantly, we were on schedule. We got our final inspection signed off on July 3, leaving me a full week to stock the kitchen and bar, and finish hiring and training the staff.

•   •   •   •   •   •   •   •   •

My partners were so pleased of what I was able to accomplish that they arranged a "date" for me, just to say thank you, for both finishing on time and to celebrate my birthday on July 7. Her name was Rachel, the same Rachel who I had been trying to connect with for years (unsuccessfully, I might add). She would visit Gatsby's Rendezvous at least twice a week and I always seemed to run into her in the places that I played in, but I hadn't been able to get past the simple flirting and an occasional cocktail.

I was ready. After all the hard work and no play, a date with a woman I have desired for years, and at thirty-five pounds lighter, to say I was ready would definitely be the understatement of the year. I picked Rachel up at around seven o'clock for dinner, but she immediately saw that I was physically exhausted; she totally understood and suggested that we skip dinner and go back to my place. She had a birthday present planned for me that she called "the silhouette."

She led me to the foot of my bed and gently started to undress me. I had no problem allowing her to take the lead, and within a few minutes, I was lying naked on my bed. With great anticipation and thoughts of a fantasy of mine being fulfilled, pure sex running through my mind, I watched Rachel as she prepared the room for my birthday present. After tuning the stereo to a soft, romantic station, she lit the candles next to my bed and attached a white sheet from the foot of my bed to the ceiling. She then set up a light several feet behind the sheet, in preparation for "the silhouette."

I was exhausted, and more than happy to let her do all the work. She started to move…gracefully, sensuously, her body flowing with the soft music behind the sheet, but in front of the light. Her "silhouette" was simply amazing, beautifully proportioned, soft lines outlining her small waist and the gentle slope of her abdomen, the movement of her breasts… *I could barely contain myself.*

She ever so slowly started to disrobe, and it was the most erotic striptease I had ever seen (and that included my short term as a bartender in a topless bar). I was lying there, completely absorbed in the moment. As she removed her last article of clothing, her lace, French-cut panties, her movements became more erotic. She moved her delicate fingers to her pubic area…*and that is the last thing I remember.* The months of construction hell and the pressure to open the lounge on time finally got the best of me, and I just passed out from total exhaustion.

Rachel woke me up the next morning and asked me to take her back to her car. I was so embarrassed, but she coyly looked at me with those big, beautiful round eyes and told me not to worry. My partners had already taken care of her fee. She enjoyed her night off and thanked me for a good night's sleep.

I'm still not sure what bothered me more, the fact that I fell asleep and didn't have sex with her or the fact that I had been too naïve to realize that for the years I had known her—*and* wanted her—that she was a professional, a prostitute, and for the entire time that I had known her, she could have been mine for the right price.

•   •   •   •   •   •   •   •   •

Our chef, Mark, was young and he came with limited experience, but he sure could cook. Only one problem: he had no freaking idea what food cost was. Liquor was my forte, not food, so it took until our bookkeeper noticed the problem before I realized anything was wrong.

We had quickly become known for great food at very reasonable prices, and we were becoming very busy, but by the end of the day, we were going broke. Our steak and shrimp dinner was awesome, and at $10.95, a great deal. Unfortunately, the actual cost of the meat: $5.00; the actual cost of the six large shrimp: $1.00 a piece; total food cost, *without* salaries and overhead: $11.00. It was as if we were running a free food kitchen. I should have stayed in the "bar" business; this food stuff was kicking my ass.

•   •   •   •   •   •   •   •   •

Libby was a strong-willed, intimidating woman in charge of the emergency room of the local hospital. As the head nurse, she spent her mornings involved with some of the most traumatic life-and-death situations imaginable. But at the end of her shift, she would make a beeline for the 770 Lounge.

The pianist had just arrived and the lounge was starting to fill up with our normal happy hour crowd when Libby arrived. It must have been tough in the emergency room that day because Libby was in a really foul mood. On a good day, she was hard to handle; on a bad day, she could put a foul-mouthed, truck-driving ex-marine to shame...and this was obviously one of those days.

The place was rocking, the piano player was "on fire," and the crowd was loving it. I looked up from my well and noticed that half my bar was lined up three deep to get a drink; the other half had only one patron: Libby. She was cutting loose on anyone within earshot, and just about every customer in the room moved as far away from her as they could get. Now, in my past life, I survived four years in the US Marine Corps with thirty-three months of combat in Vietnam. I considered myself relatively fearless, but when Libby was on a roll, I was scared to death (and I had no doubt that physically, she could kick my ass).

As the bartender, I had to make a quick decision: talk Libby into a calmer state or ask her to leave the bar. I had determined that I would take the forceful approach (there were a couple of dozen regular customers at the bar who would have loved to jump her if she came after me...I was feeling almost safe). "Libby," I commanded, "sit down and shut up. You paid $2.20 for your drink. That bought you twenty-two inches of space. Now, sit down. I don't want you looking left; I don't want you looking right. You sit there, drink your drink, leave the other customers alone, and keep your damn mouth shut... and I expect a better tip when you leave. Any questions?"

I still have no idea why, but she did exactly what I told her to do. When the stool at the far end of the bar opened up, I moved Libby over so that she would have a little more room and she would be a little farther from the rest of the crowd, but she was behaving. She did seem to physically calm down, just a touch, and I was amazed when she politely requested another drink. When she finished it, she stood up, left a $5 tip, and disappeared into the night. (Up to this point of our relationship, she had never left more than a couple of bucks.)

* * *   * * *   * * *

It was a Saturday afternoon and my bar was empty. The only customer entertaining me was Libby. The back door opened and in walked an elderly couple who looked as if they walked right out of the "Ma and Pa Kettle on the farm" picture. The only thing missing were the bales of hay in the background and Pa's pitchfork. Naturally, they had to sit next to Libby (there were *only* twenty-one additional empty bar stools, but the two next to Libby were obviously the better choice). "Pa Kettle" had just ordered a beer for himself and a margarita for his wife when Libby opened her mouth with a few choice adjectives. I immediately leaned over to remind her of our past conversations and to keep her mouth shut.

Well, I guess "Ma Kettle" took *huge* offense with both my tone of voice and my attitude. "How dare you speak to a woman in that tone of voice? That's disgusting. You should be ashamed of yourself. A real man would never use that kind of language when talking to a lady."

And just at that exact moment, Libby spun around, looked at the formidable "Ma Kettle," and exclaimed, "Shut the fuck up, Bitch. He knows what he's doing."

Well, "Pa Kettle" lost it. He was laughing so hard that he spilled his drink. "Ma Kettle" was speechless, and was either too embarrassed or too mad, but she just got up and left the bar. They must have been kindred spirits, because after "Pa Kettle" composed himself, he and Libby spent the rest of the afternoon drinking and telling dirty jokes…as "Ma Kettle" sat diligently in their car, waiting for Pa.

● ● ●　　● ● ●　　● ● ●

The 770 Lounge had been open for two months when I received a call from the wife of a longtime customer and friend. Chris had been diagnosed with terminal cancer; he had moved to Las Vegas a year earlier, so I arranged for the weekend off, invited a mutual friend of ours, and made plans to visit.

I pulled into the parking lot to pick Breanna up, a tall, beautifully proportioned woman with long, brown hair and outrageously large, voluptuous breasts. She was a bartender at a local Italian *ristorante* in Riverside, and anyone who had had the sheer joy of watching her work realized that she effectively "owned the bar." Customers would drive for many miles just for the privilege of having her pour them a few cocktails, and I had been one of them. My friend Chris and I would drive over an hour, at least twice a week, just to admire, but this time, it was different. Breanna and I were going to Las Vegas together to say good-bye to our friend Chris. I had been trying for over a year to hook up with Breanna, offering trips to Vegas, long weekends to San Francisco, but she never mixed business with pleasure, and as long as I was a customer of hers, it would always be business. It took our friend's misfortune for us to finally spend some time together away from her bar.

We arrived in Las Vegas at around noon, but because Chris was in so much pain, and on some pretty intense medication, we weren't going to be able to see him until later that night. We spent a little time walking around the downtown area and then went back to the hotel for a quick nap. It was a big room, with two beds…and I *still* wasn't able to convince her to mix business with pleasure.

As we were about to start the evening, I watched her getting ready, first her shower, then makeup, and finally slipping into a very elegant, form-fitting red dress. It was strapless, and when she saw my amazement of how the top stayed up around those magnificent breasts, she shared with me the secret of the double-sided tape that was used to cover both her very prominent nipples and keep the dress from falling—*that damn 3M company.*

As we entered the casino, I noticed a couple of spots about to open on a busy crap table, and when I asked her if she would be interested, she replied, "I've never played." Now I'm old school, and *really* excited. A beautiful "virgin" on the crap table; we couldn't lose. I slid us between two very large gentlemen and the entire table stopped for a moment to stare. As I said, they were "magnificent."

Now, it should be noted that for the gamblers of Las Vegas, nothing, not an earthquake, not the implosion of a strip casino, not even the July 4 bicentennial fireworks, nothing stops a Las Vegas gambler from making a bet… nothing, it seemed, except Breanna's arrival. I placed our bets on the pass line, but when the dealer offered the dice to "Bre," she refused. She was just too nervous. She ordered a double martini from the waitress and watched as the dice worked their way around the table. As they came to her again, she once again "passed the dice" and ordered another double martini. As she was finishing her third double martini, the dice made it around to her again, but this time, she looked up and said, "Give me those fucking dice."

After a few moments of silence, the elderly dealer sitting in the position of power on the table looked up at her, then at me, and said, "Well, give her the fucking dice!"

Almost immediately, everyone on the table started to double their bets, and as she threw the dice down the length of the table, everyone cheered; her large breasts seemed to leap out at everyone, but the tape held, and she rolled an eleven, a winner. Breanna held the dice for only a few minutes, but by the time we left the table, all three dealers and the pit boss made sure that she left with their phone numbers and a promise to call.

• • •   • • •   • • •

I had made a few dollars while "Bre" held the dice, but it was getting late, so we decided to go to the restaurant to wait for Chris and his wife. It was quickly approaching eight and our reservations were for nine. Hugo's was located inside the Four Queens Hotel, just off the casino floor, and as we took the few steps down from the main level, we were in another world. It was very dark, with a small, six-stool bar to the left and several small isolated dining areas to the right. The room was very intimate, and to add to the dining experience, the servers were using "cart service," preparing much of the food at the table.

While we were waiting to be seated, we sat at the bar and ordered a bottle of wine. Then all of a sudden, we heard a gasp from our neighbors to the left. As the four of them called to Breanna (four of *her* regular customers from the Italian *ristorante* just happened to be in Vegas, and all "Bre" could think about was that they would go back and tell her boyfriend that they saw her having dinner in Las Vegas with some Italian-looking guy).

As our neighbors were shown to their table, I started telling the bartender about how great it had been to work on Catalina Island. After a couple of years of bartending in paradise, I had left the island, and my employers, Barry and Pat, got a divorce. Barry moved to Las Vegas and worked as a bartender at this very same Four Queens and eventually moved in with a new girlfriend, a waitress working at the Sands Hotel. Pat stayed on the island, and eventually married her bartender, my friend Jimmy. About a week after Barry left the island, I went to Vegas to spend the weekend with him, his new girlfriend, and her teenage son. Barry and his new girlfriend were married a year later.

As I was sharing a few of my great Catalina stories with our bartender, our waiter joined in. He had also worked on the island for a couple of years and had known my ex-boss, Barry, intimately. Our waiter for the evening? It was Barry's stepson, the teenager I had met years earlier. *Our friend Chris better show up soon, before anyone else recognizes us.*

• • •   • • •   • •

Dinner was great, but Chris had no stamina. Between the drugs and the treatment, he was only able to function in four-hour increments, four hours of sleep, four hours awake, all day long. We said good night and went back to our room, and with just a little coaxing, Breanna agreed to a massage...*finally*. She removed her dress and laid face down on the bed, in just her red G-string, and I stripped down to my briefs and reached for the lotion in my bag.

Slowly, ever so slowly, I worked her long, tanned body, starting at her feet and then moving up. I worked on her for almost three hours, making sure that I covered her entire body—*and I was very thorough*. It was painfully obvious that I was in a very excited state, and as I moved off her and slid into my own bed, I looked over and said, "Bre, if you glance over during the middle of the night and see me waiving at you, it won't be my hands. Please let me know if you would like me to come back and finish the job."

Damn, she was tough, and she kept it business…even after we returned home. I spent the next several years trying to finish the job, but to no avail. When Breanna and I received the call, Chris had been given less than six months to live, but with the help of his great wife, countless vitamins, and a complete change to an organic and vegan lifestyle, he lived for another two years…*and will always continue to live in my heart.*

· · ·   · · ·   · · ·

The lounge had been opened for several months when I met Kathy; almost five feet nothing and about 100 pounds, she was a stunning beauty and way out of my league. She carried herself with class, her makeup was always perfect, and her outfits were always designer labels. But there were two things that really made her stand out in a crowd: she would always wear a stylish hat and she had the brightest, "ice blue" eyes that I had ever seen.

As fate would have it, four weeks and an awful lot of free drinks later (not that a bartender *ever* gives away a drink), Kathy asked me to spend the weekend with her in her new condo. We woke up on Sunday morning after spending the entire day before in bed. She was beautiful, the conversation was meaningless, but the sex was good—not great, not earth shattering, just good. I was just about to ask her if she would like to join me at a friend's grand opening of his liquor store that afternoon when she asked me how old I was. When I told her, she got this inquisitive look on her face and asked to see my driver's license. She looked at mine and immediately went to get hers; we were born on the exact same day, and apparently, only minutes apart. Obviously, this relationship was just meant to be, our timing was perfect, the stars were aligned, and we would have a beautiful future together. *Did I mention that she believed in that sort of thing?*

I served us breakfast in bed, but when I started to get ready for my friend's party, she rolled over and went back to sleep. She wouldn't know anyone at the party and she decided to rest up for tonight's activities. She was fast asleep when I left.

· · ·   · · ·   · · ·

Our hosts for the party had been regular customers of mine and Joe P.'s for years, both while we were working at Rooney's Restaurant and Lorenzo's.

We both thought it our obligation to support them with their new venture. The party was located at a pool and spa showroom, next to the liquor store that our friends were opening. It was an excellent setting. The room was filled with waterfalls and spas, giving the feel of a garden party, but it was indoors.

"Sam," as she now preferred to be called, was standing with her parents, Hack and Doreen, our hosts, enjoying a cocktail, when both Joe P. and I noticed her. Slight of build, wearing glasses, her hair was up off her face, she was dressed casually, but it was immediately obvious to both of us that she had a great pair of legs and a face to die for.

It had been years since I saw her last, and the few times when she had joined her parents, Hack and Doreen, for dinner at Lorenzo's were only memorable for me...not her. For me, it was love at first sight, but I was with Joe P. I had accepted my fate as his wingman long ago. He had the looks and the lines, and when he wanted to be charming, I didn't stand a chance. He took one look at "Sam" and decided to be charming; I guess I would have to wait to find the future mother of my children.

As the party was coming to an end, I suggested that we continue the celebration at the 770 Lounge. I had hired a jazz trio to perform on Sunday afternoons and the place should be fun. The minute we walked in, I knew there was something not quite right. It was quiet for just a moment, then it hit us: the jazz trio I hired had decided to invite some of their entertainer friends to join them, and there they were...all twenty-two of them, filling the stage *and* the dance floor.

I could see the look of pain on Joe P.'s face. He was a die-hard country western fan, and this was like a poison dart jabbing into his brain. Now I like soft, easy listening, smooth jazz, but when twenty-two musicians get together to "jam," there is nothing soft, easy, or smooth about it; they all seemed to be in their own little world, and all of them were playing something different. There are many adjectives that one could use to describe the type of "music" being played on my stage, but only one came to mind at that moment: *painful*.

My guests were also my friends, and with the help of numerous cocktails, we managed to survive the afternoon. I had spent the entire time fantasizing about Sam and was just starting to imagine what my friend Kathy had in store for me when Joe P. stood up and announced that he was leaving. The music had finally gotten to him. He glanced over at me and said, "The hell with it. You can have her," and left. I looked over at Sam and the other couple who had survived the day and invited them all to join me for dinner. Kathy would wait up for me.

The four of us had a great time, Curt and Jean, old customers and friends, had an anniversary coming up, so we used that dinner to help them celebrate.

After several cocktails, Sam and I were feeling pretty comfortable together, and as we were leaving the restaurant, I asked her out for dinner for the next day; she accepted.

• •   •   •   •   •   •   •   •

I wanted to make a good first impression for our first "date," so I arrived about thirty minutes early. I parked my '68 Corvette around the corner from Sam's house and took the top down to catch some rays. I wasn't there five minutes when Sam came up to me wearing just a light robe, with her hair in curlers. She was frantic. One of her dogs had escaped from the backyard and she needed to find him before we left. I told her to go finish getting ready and that I would take care of it. The dog, an Irish setter named Toma, was just a big cuddly bear and wouldn't hurt a fly, so Sam went back into the house and I started my search. I had just turned my car onto the very next street and there he was, on the front porch of the house in front of me. I pulled over, walked around to the passenger side of my car, and opened the door. "Toma, get in the car."

Years later, it still amazes me that Toma just walked up to the car, stepped in, and sat down on the passenger seat. The top was off my car, and this dog just sat there, catching some rays. I liked him immediately. I pulled into Sam's driveway, got out, and opened the car door for him. He just walked up to the front door and damn near let himself in. *Pretty good start for a first date.*

• •   •   •   •   •   •   •   •

The next day, I picked her up at her office and took her to lunch, and then we made plans for dinner that night. We spent every day, for the next several weeks, together, and in all that time, I had barely been able to steal a kiss. I was in love, and I told her so, but she wasn't going to make it that easy for me. *Oh, and I never did see "ice blue eyes" again.*

When we finally had sex, it was natural. Everything we did, the conversations, the sex, all of our time together, was natural. It was as if this was truly meant to be. About a month after Sam and I started dating, I asked her to marry me, and she accepted. But only if I promised not to go to Vegas for at least two years (obviously, I had given her too much information about my previous Vegas trips). She would spend the next eighteen months making sure that I was ready to settle down, but at least she had said yes. I also knew that there wasn't a chance in hell that I could be a faithful husband if I stayed a bartender, so I decided to use our engagement period to make a career change. After ten years in the "business," it was time.

Seven Ways to Treat a Lady • 121

For the entire time that I have known him, Joe P. *always* wound up with the girl. It could be said that it was fate, or that it was just meant to be. But in my heart, I know that the reason Joe left that afternoon, the reason that I met and fell in love with this woman, the reason I eventually married her, was because of *bad jazz.*

A young teen decided that it was time to lose his virginity, and he wanted it to be with a woman who could teach him, so he propositioned a friend of his father's, a local prostitute.

As she entered the room, the prostitute took off her clothes and lied back on the bed; she then told the boy to take his clothes off and kneel between her legs. He did as he was instructed.

A few minutes later, she told him to put a finger in her vagina. He was nervous, and a little scared, but he did what he was told. As he started to have a little fun, she told him to put a second finger in, and then a third, and as all good students do, he did what he was told. Then she told him to put his whole hand in—and he did.

As he was pumping his hand into her vagina, and with each thrust, she called out, "Now. Put. Your. Other. Hand in."

He looked up in shock, but he complied. After all, that was why he hired her, to teach him what to do.

It was a struggle, but eventually, he was able to squeeze in both hands. The seasoned old pro smiled down at her young protégé and proclaimed, "Tight, huh?"

Epilogue

• • •   • • •   • • •

I was just starting to accept my new profession as a loan officer for a small mortgage company, but it had been a tough transition, and I only had six months before Sam and I would be married. One of the prerequisites to becoming a loan officer in the State of California was to have a real estate license, and I was having trouble with that. The Department of Real Estate offered classes and a final exam, but you had to get 105 answers right, out of 150 questions. If you fail the exam, they would tell you how many questions you got right; if you pass, they just tell you congratulations in a very simple form letter. On my first test, I had 104 right answers; three weeks later, on my second attempt, I had 104 right answers; no license, no career change. Bartending I knew and loved; it was easy for me, and as I was just starting to doubt this whole career move thing, I got a call from a voice from my past.

Keith, my lead bartender from the Gatsby's Rendezvous days, had referred me to his father, the new owner of the Landmark Hotel and Casino in Las Vegas. I was asked to fly out for the weekend and all expenses would be taken care of. I thought it prudent to invite Sam, even though she was *not* a fan of Vegas.

A limousine picked us up at our house in Irvine and took us to a private plane waiting for us at the John Wayne Airport. From the moment we landed in Vegas, we were treated like royalty; everything had been taken care of by the management of the hotel...*everything*. I had been asked my opinion on how to remodel the restaurant located on top of the tower in front of the hotel (for years, it was the tallest structure in Vegas and it was considered *the* landmark of Las Vegas, one that the "world" recognized).

The remodeling had to be perfect, and I was working with both management and their advisors on how I thought it should be designed, and after two days, they made me an offer: food and beverage manager of the Landmark Hotel and Casino. Pretty damn impressive. I would be considered upper management, bypass the time restraints imposed by the culinary union for employment opportunities in Vegas, and start at a very high salary. *Essentially, my fantasy was about to become reality.*

As I turned to my fiancée, she looked incredulously at me and said quietly, "Well, Honey, it's a good thing that we love each other, because with you in Las Vegas and me in Irvine, it's going to be one hell of a marriage."

As I said, she was not a fan, and it didn't take me long to take the hint.

Back in California, on my third attempt at the real estate exam, I had 103 right answers…the ego was shot, I was going backward, and I was starting to doubt the whole marriage thing, when Sam convinced me to try one last time. I studied my ass off, and when I was done, I received the simple form letter: I had passed. I was out of time, the wedding was in a couple of months, and my new real estate license insured the start of my new career.

But it was okay, everything happens for a reason; managing the restaurant on top of the tallest structure in Las Vegas would have been a huge problem. I was afraid of heights.

A priest and a rabbi just finished checking into heaven, and as they entered through the pearly gates, they were approached by a tall, white-haired, gentle soul by the name of Jonathan. He introduced himself as the one responsible for giving them their housing assignments.

As the three of them started a tour, both the priest and the rabbi were getting very excited. Thanks to their lifetime of devotion and worship, they were headed to the street that God lived on.

As they turned onto the street, they noticed that it was dominated by the largest home they had ever seen. His house was white, of course, but it had beautifully crafted sculptures everywhere…it was awe inspiring.

*As they walked along the street, Jonathan would point out the homes that were available. The closer they got to **His** house, the more excited they became, but by the time they reached the end, they hadn't decided on anything…until, that is, they were in front of **His** gate.*

Simultaneously, both the priest and the rabbi pointed to the little white house off to the left of God's place (it was, after all, the right hand of God's) and proclaimed, "We want that one."

But Jonathan sadly informed them, "Sorry, that one is no longer available. It's reserved."

They both begged and pleaded, but to no avail.

"Sorry, not going to happen. Joe P. should be arriving any day now, and God's personal bartender gets whatever he wants."

Seven Ways to Treat a Lady

Confessions of a Bartender

• • • • • • • • •

When I decided to become a professional bartender, it was during the age of innocence. The Vietnam "conflict" had divided a nation, laws were less complicated, the attitude of Mothers Against Drunk Drivers was in it's infancy, and AIDS had not been discovered yet; it was a different generation. More alcohol, more fun, more sex...with few distractions and even fewer consequences.

I was young, I had bills to pay, a personal life I was trying to enjoy, and I chose bartending as a profession...

• • • • • • • •

I gazed into her eyes, her bloodshot, puffy eyes, and asked her how she did it. How could she possibly be even more beautiful than the last time I saw her?

And the arrogant, more than slightly drunk sitting next to her, hopefully, will tip, because serving him and his obnoxious group is far from being fun.

I'm a professional bartender... I get paid to do a job, to be nice, and to serve, but really, there are only two reasons to be a bartender: to get paid or to get laid. And with a little luck, you may get both.

• • • • • • • •